IDENTITY THEFT

Private Battle or Public Crisis?

Rachael Hanel and Erin L. McCoy

Cavendish Square

New York

Published in 2019 by Cavendish Square Publishing, LLC
243 5th Avenue, Suite 136, New York, NY 10016

Website: cavendishsq.com

This publication represents the opinions and views of the author based on his or her personal
experience, knowledge, and research. The information in this book serves as a general guide
only. The author and publisher have used their best efforts in preparing this book and disclaim
liability rising directly or indirectly from the use and application of this book.

All websites were available and accurate when this book was sent to press.

Library of Congress Cataloging-in-Publication Data

Names: Hanel, Rachael, author. | McCoy, Erin L., author.
Title: Identity theft : private battle or public crisis? / Rachael Hanel and Erin L. McCoy.
Description: First Edition. | New York : Cavendish Square, [2019] |
Series: Today's debates | Audience: Grades 7-12. | Includes bibliographical references and index.
Identifiers: LCCN 2018012345 (print) | LCCN 2018013370 (ebook) |
ISBN 9781502643247 (ebook) | ISBN 9781502643230 (library bound) |
ISBN 9781502643223 (pbk.)Subjects: LCSH: Identity theft--Juvenile literature. |
Identity theft--Prevention--Juvenile literature.
Classification: LCC HV6675 (ebook) | LCC HV6675 .H286 2019 (print) | DDC 364.16/33--dc23
LC record available at https://lccn.loc.gov/2018012345

Editorial Director: David McNamara
Copy Editor: Rebecca Rohan
Associate Art Director: Alan Sliwinski
Production Coordinator: Karol Szymczuk
Photo Research: J8 Media

The photographs in this book are used by permission and through the courtesy of: Cover, Direk Yiamsaensuk/
Shutterstock.com; p. 4 Swedish Marble/Shutterstock.com; p. 7 Dennizn/ Shutterstock.com; pp. 10, 54
Mark Van Scyoc/Shutterstock.com; p. 15 Rowman & Littlefield Publishers; p. 17 National Archives-
JFK/Corbis/Getty Images; p. 21 Social Security Administration/File: Social security card john q public.
png/Wikimedia Commons/Public Domain; p. 25 Hernandez/MCT/Newscom; p. 26 (top) Bacho/
Shutterstock.com, (bottom) YP_photographer/Shutterstock.com; p. 29 Monkey Business Images/
Shutterstock.com; p. 33 ROBYN BECK/AFP/Getty Images; p. 37 Infrogmation, Own work/File:
Low9Debris3.jpg/Wikimedia Commons/CCA 2.5 Generic license; p. 38 Mike Harrington/DigitalVision/
Getty Images; p. 42 Maxx-Studio/Shutterstock.com; p. 43 Iakov Filimonov/Shutterstock.com; p. 48
Stock_photo_world/Shutterstock.com; pp. 51, 70 Rawpixel.com/Shutterstock.com; p. 56 Ronnie Chua/
Shutterstock.com; p. 61 Fizkes/Shutterstock.com; p. 63 (L) AP Photo/Lucy Nicholson, (R) Everett
Collection, Inc./Alamy Stock Photo; p. 75 Krunja/Shutterstock.com; p. 82 Jacob Lund/Shutterstock.com;
p. 94 Seksan Mongkhonkhamsao/Moment/Getty Images; p. 100 Alfred Pasieka/ Science Photo Library/
Getty Images; p. 104 Anthony Devlin/PA/AP Photo; p. 109 Artyom Korotayev/TASS/ Getty Images.

Printed in the United States of America

CONTENTS

INTRODUCTION

Art Damiao's identity theft nightmare began with a single phone call in 2017. When Damiao, an IT specialist, answered the phone, the person on the other end of the line had his Social Security number, his driver's license number, and control over his email account. The thief demanded a ransom in exchange for relinquishing control of Damiao's online profiles: $300 in Bitcoin, a digital currency. "I can basically pretend to be you right now. I am you," the thief told him, according to a CBS News article. Meanwhile, Damiao watched, helpless, as the hacker attempted to change the passwords for his Amazon, eBay, and bank accounts.

Opposite: One kind of malware is ransomware, a program that holds a person's personal information hostage until a ransom is paid.

Damiao refused to pay the ransom, and he eventually regained access to and control of his identity. However, as in so many cases of identity theft, it's hard to know how his information was stolen in the first place, making it difficult to determine how to prevent similar scenarios in the future. Damiao has his suspicions, though. He was among 145.5 million Americans who were left vulnerable to identity theft after a data breach at Equifax, one of the United States' three biggest credit-reporting agencies, was discovered on July 29, 2017.

Big Breaches, Big Losses

Identity theft is a crime in which someone steals your personal information, such as your credit card number or your Social Security number. The thief can then use this information to open up credit card accounts or bank accounts in your name, steal your money, and/or impersonate you. Few people realize how much information is compiled about them and how it is used. Banks, credit card companies, employers, and government agencies are just a few of the organizations that keep personal data on file. With the vast amount of information out there, it is no wonder that this data sometimes falls into the wrong hands.

The Equifax breach was certainly not the only large-scale identity theft in US history. In 2015, the US Department of the Interior and the Office of Personnel Management were breached, compromising the records of 22 million current and past government employees. Large companies have likewise been targeted. That same year, the data of 90 million customers was exposed after the data of two health insurance companies—Premera Blue Cross and Anthem—was breached. In 2014, 145 million eBay users' information was compromised. Three billion Yahoo users have been compromised over the years. A 2013 cyberattack on the big-box retailer Target exposed 41 million

Equifax, one of the three largest credit-reporting agencies in the United States, suffered a massive data breach in 2017.

credit card accounts; in response to a class-action lawsuit, Target agreed to pay $18.5 million to affected customers. These breaches, alongside small-scale thefts—sometimes perpetrated by members of a victim's own family—are impacting upwards of fifteen million Americans every year.

Investigating Identity Theft

How to protect consumers' personal data, and who is responsible for doing so, is an ongoing controversy among regulatory and law enforcement agencies. The Equifax case provides a prime example. By February 2018, the Consumer Financial Protection Bureau (CFPB), a US government agency, had reportedly scaled back its investigation into the Equifax hack. It had not sought routine testimony or subpoenas of executives, and it had decided not to pursue tests of Equifax's methods of protecting data. Other government agencies, such as the Federal Trade Commission, were still investigating the breach, but many were concerned at the lack of governmental oversight. More than 240 class-action lawsuits had been filed against the company, and now it seemed that these might be the only means for consumers to seek justice or retribution for the losses they had suffered.

A *Los Angeles Times* columnist called the CFPB's approach "an act of madness." *Forbes* contributor Tony Bradley argued that "[g]overnment apathy and a lack of consequences underscore why cybersecurity continues to be such a major issue." Bradley added that consumers have no choice as to whether to share their personal information with credit bureaus such as Equifax, making it the government's responsibility to investigate:

> *The credit bureaus are essentially industry and government sanctioned identity theft—capturing and storing all of your most sensitive personal data without your authorization ... At least when Target or Home Depot get breached, the data they have is a result of a decision consumers made, and those consumers can choose to take their business elsewhere if they don't feel like those companies are adequately safeguarding their personal data.*

This and similar controversies get to the heart of the identity-theft debate. Who is responsible for investigating identity theft and for ensuring that attackers are brought to justice? "The Equifax breach exposed vulnerabilities in how the companies keep data safe. It also highlighted how credit bureaus exist in a regulatory gray zone where they are partly regulated by several agencies," wrote Reuters reporter Patrick Rucker on February 4, 2018.

Meanwhile, many consumers and regulators are worried that there aren't sufficient regulations in place to ensure that companies handle such breaches appropriately. Equifax, for instance, waited about six weeks before it publicly disclosed the breach. US senator Elizabeth Warren, who launched her own investigation into the breach, accused Equifax of trying to "wiggle off the hook."

"For years, Equifax and other big credit reporting agencies have been able to get away with profiting off using people's private info and doing so without their explicit permission," Warren said. "We need real consequences for when they screw up." She insisted that the credit-bureau industry should be "completely transformed." However, such regulations would not address the multitude of large-scale breaches that have occurred across industries in the past several years. Who will make key decisions about regulating and enforcing penalties for such breaches is in many ways still a matter of debate.

UNITED STATES

FEDERAL
TRADE
COMMISSION
BUILDING

Chapter One

DEFINING IDENTITY THEFT

A total of 16.7 million US consumers lost $16.8 billion to identity theft in 2017, up 8 percent from the previous year. It was a record high, with 6.6 percent of American consumers falling victim to the crime. According to a joint report published by the Center for Strategic and International Studies and McAfee (a computer security software company), losses due to cybercrime ranged between $375 and $575 billion on a global scale in 2014.

What is identity theft, and what makes it so harmful to those affected? Simply put, identity theft is the unlawful use of someone else's personal information. This private data can be used to secure credit, make purchases, obtain medical services, get jobs, or evade criminal

Opposite: Pictured is the Federal Trade Commission (FTC) headquarters in Washington, DC.

investigation. This is not an exhaustive list; there are many reasons that someone would steal another person's identity.

Identity theft is on the rise. Between 2013 and 2016, complaints of this crime to the Consumer Sentinel Network, which is maintained by the Federal Trade Commission (FTC), increased by 37.6 percent. The year 2017 saw a new record, with the number of breaches in the United States increasing 44.7 percent from 2016.

The History of Identity Theft

Technology makes our lives easier in many ways. We can quickly make purchases, obtain credit, and check bank statements over the internet. Unfortunately, this technology also makes it easier for thieves to steal information. This is why identity theft is a growing problem.

However, identity theft is not new. Scheming thieves have always found ways to steal other people's identities for the purpose of avoiding their own crimes or for financial gain. In 1923, a New Orleans man named Harry Wolfe was canoeing with a friend, Jacob Arnof, when Arnof drowned. Wolfe did not report the death to police. Instead, he assumed Arnof's identity, even going so far as to mark his own face to mimic a scar that Arnof bore. Wolfe posed as Arnof to send messages to Arnof's father and obtain money from family bank accounts. Wolfe eventually confessed to his identity theft scheme.

When the telephone became more common in the twentieth century, thieves used the new technology to obtain personal information. One common scam involved calling people to tell them that they had won a prize. The caller would tell the victim that he or she needed to share personal information, such as a Social Security number or date of birth, in order to claim the prize. The caller then had enough information to create a financial account using the newly obtained name.

Another common identity-theft technique that has been around for a long time is to rifle through someone's mail or trash. A mailbox can contain a wealth of personal information, from billing statements to credit card offers. If unwanted mail is thrown away intact, someone going through the garbage may find account statements and addresses. This low-tech way of gathering personal information, called "dumpster diving," is so reliable that thieves still use it today.

Another tried-and-true method for stealing information is to grab someone's wallet or purse, which often contains credit cards, a driver's license, a Social Security number, and blank checks—enough information to get a thief well on his or her way to assuming a new identity.

Today, online storage of vast databases of information has made millions of people vulnerable to identity theft. For their part, thieves continue to develop more and more ways to hack into these databases. With the advent of the "dark web" (an online marketplace where people buy and sell illegal goods and services), it is now easier than ever for hackers and thieves to sell the information that they've stolen. In 2017, Social Security numbers were available for as little as $1 apiece on the dark web. You could buy a driver's license number for $20, or a person's complete medical record for $1,000.

Who Is at Risk?

Identity theft can strike anyone at any time. No one is immune to this crime. However, reports suggest that certain populations and age groups are more susceptible than others.

Children

Children are at particular risk for identity theft. Robert P. Chappell Jr., author of the book *Child Identity Theft: What You Need to Know*, estimates that 1.3 million children are impacted by identity theft each year; half of those children are younger than six. In 2017, credit-reporting agency Experian reported that 17 percent of the fraud cases it handled each year targeted children. In fact, Experian's vice president of consumer protection told financial services firm Morgan Stanley that one in four children were likely to be affected by identity theft or fraud by the time they reach the age of eighteen. These are startling figures.

A child's identity can be compromised in a number of ways. In some cases, parents use their children's Social Security numbers to obtain credit cards or set up utility services. Credit card applications are easy to fill out. Applicants fill in a name, address, and Social Security number, and often no one verifies the age or identity of the applicant. Meanwhile, as more and more children access the internet regularly, they may themselves share personal information without knowing the impact such sharing may have. All of these factors open the door to identity theft.

Thieves target children for two reasons: first, they have a fresh credit history, and second, it can take years before anyone discovers the crime. It is only when the child grows older and applies for credit cards and school or car loans that many such thefts are uncovered. Zach Friesen, for example, was seventeen years old when a prospective employer ran a credit report on him and discovered he was $40,000 in debt. Someone had stolen Friesen's identity when he was seven years old, used his name to buy a large boat, and never paid the loan. Friesen later built a career traveling around the country to educate teens and other young adults about the dangers of identity theft.

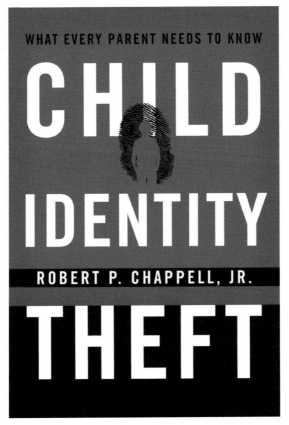

More than one million children are affected by identity theft every year, according to Robert P. Chappell, Jr.

Parents and guardians should be aware of warning signs that someone may be using a child's identity. For example, the child may start receiving credit card applications, bills, or bank statements in the mail. Debt collectors might call and ask to speak to the child. Or, when the time comes for an older child to finally open an account, there may be one already open at a bank in his or her name.

As children start using the internet, the FTC also recommends talking to them about how to protect their identities online.

Kids should understand the importance of keeping their personal information private and maintaining strong passwords for their online accounts. They should also be taught to be suspicious of popups, phishing emails and text messages, downloads from insecure sites, and promises for "free" things like games and downloads.

The Elderly

In 2014, 2.6 million elderly Americans were victims of identity theft, according to the US Department of Justice's Bureau of Justice Statistics. US senator Susan Collins has called such fraud against older Americans "a growing epidemic," and in 2018, a bill she authored to protect seniors from such exploitation was making its way through Congress. The Senior $afe Act was designed to "provide support to regulators, financial institutions, and legal organizations to educate their employees about how to identify and prevent financial exploitation of older Americans."

The elderly can be more vulnerable than most to identity theft, especially to theft perpetrated by caregivers or adult children. There are legal measures in place to prevent this. For older people who are losing mental capabilities, including the ability to handle and understand their own finances, a court will often appoint a legal guardian. The guardian is usually a family member or a close friend. However, this arrangement can open the doors to financial abuse. Guardians have access to all of the person's personal and financial data, and can easily use his or her Social Security number or fill out credit-card applications that come in the mail without anyone else knowing about it. Elderly people with cognitive incapacities can suffer 100 percent greater losses than those without such disabilities.

The National Center on Elder Abuse reports that financial abuse costs elderly Americans more than $2.6 billion every year. Identity theft perpetrated against elders by relatives or trusted friends may be one of the most underreported forms of identity theft. Victims are often reluctant to pursue criminal charges against family members. They may think that somehow it is their fault. Seeing a child go to jail can add stress to an already stressful and confusing time.

The Dead

Another group targeted by identity thieves are the recently deceased. Criminals scour obituary notices online and in newspapers and may attempt to take over the identity of someone who has just died. They call widows or widowers claiming to be medical facility representatives and ask for Social Security numbers and birth dates to "finalize paperwork." Criminals use a dead person's Social Security number for all the same reasons they use a living person's data: to buy goods, secure credit, and get jobs. In the case of obtaining employment, people may never discover that a false Social Security number has been used as long as taxes are paid on the wages earned.

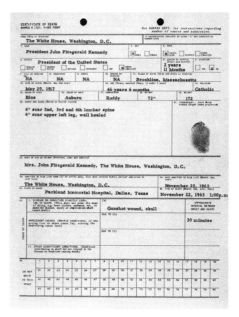

This is an example of a death certificate, which can be used by identity thieves.

Thieves steal dead people's identities because it is hard to detect: the actual victim cannot alert authorities. Stealing the identity of the deceased does not harm that person, but it can harm relatives left behind. Creditors may eventually come after the relatives, seeking payment on unpaid charges. Relatives are then responsible for resolving the situation. It can cause them financial and psychological harm during a difficult period.

College Students

A 2014 survey found that students are more likely than other groups to experience a significant impact when they become the victims of identity theft. Yet they are also the least likely group to detect such theft themselves, being three times more likely than the average victim to learn about a fraud from someone else, such as a debt collector. What's more, students are four times more likely to be victimized by someone they know.

College students can be easy targets for a number of reasons. For one, they may not know much about managing their finances or about identity theft and how to protect themselves. They are also of a generation that has always been comfortable sharing their personal information online, whether they're taking tests, making purchases, surfing social networks, or filling out job applications.

Students' names and personal information can be found in all types of college and university databases and in federal loan databases, and such databases have been compromised again and again. In 2017, Washington State University sent letters to one million people whose information was jeopardized after a hard drive was stolen. That same year, the personal information of as many as one hundred thousand people was reported stolen when a tool for filling out the Free Application for Federal Student Aid (FAFSA) was breached.

College students are frequent targets of credit card companies, and this can put them at risk too. When they walk through their student union buildings, they often are bombarded with requests from credit-card company representatives to fill out applications. Sitting next to those legitimate companies may be scammers waiting to pounce and obtain a student's personal information. College students frequently receive credit card offers in the mail as well. If they throw away the offers without shredding them, someone going through the trash can steal and fill out the applications.

Highly Active Web Users

People who share a lot of their information online, whether on websites or through ostensibly secure platforms, may be at higher risk, a 2017 report conducted by Javelin Strategy & Research found. The study pointed to three groups in particular: social networkers, online shoppers, and what it called "digitally connected consumers."

Why are people who are especially active on social networks such as Facebook, Instagram, and Snapchat at risk? People on these platforms share a lot of information about themselves: their name, their location, their spending habits. Thieves can compile and use this personal information to impersonate an individual or access his or her accounts. Social networkers are at a 46 percent–higher risk of their accounts being taken over by thieves, Javelin reported.

Online shoppers share a great deal of financial information when they make purchases on the web. More than 60 percent of those shoppers surveyed by Javelin in 2017 had made an online purchase in the last week. Sharing their credit or debit card information online resulted in a higher risk of that information falling into the wrong hands. Digitally connected consumers— people who spend more time on social networks, shopping online, and interacting with mobile devices—are at a 30 percent–higher risk of fraud. On a positive note, however, online shoppers are more likely to catch fraud early and minimize its impact, whereas consumers with little online presence are more likely to take forty-plus days to detect fraud.

Businesses

Not only are individuals at risk, but so are businesses. Individuals are a source of just one set of personal data. On the other hand, a business can store hundreds, thousands, or even hundreds of thousands of names and account numbers in one central database. Thieves greedily hope to capitalize on this wealth of data. Data breaches cost businesses $225 per stolen record for an average total of $7.35 million per breach, according to a 2017 Ponemon Institute report. It took businesses an average of 206 days to detect and fifty-five days to contain data breach incidents in 2017, meaning that data was often exposed for the better part of a year.

Much of the personal information that businesses document can be stolen at the workplace. Workplace identity theft can occur in many ways, such as an unethical human resources worker perusing records, a janitor rifling through papers dumped in the trash, or a hacker gaining access to employee records, for instance.

Businesses themselves can be the targets of identity thieves. Businesses are assigned a variety of identification numbers, just as individuals are. These numbers include federal employer identification numbers, Department of the Treasury numbers, and tax identification numbers. Business numbers are used the same way individual numbers are: to access existing accounts or to open new ones.

How Identity Theft Occurs

Just as physical characteristics—such as hair color, eye color, and height—make each person unique, every person has a set of data that is unique to him or her. If this information falls into the wrong hands, it can allow a thief to assume someone else's identity for criminal purposes. Here is a closer look at what type of information is vulnerable to thieves.

Social Security Numbers

Upon birth, citizenship, or permanent residency, the US Social Security Administration assigns everyone a nine-digit Social Security number. The government uses this number for tax

Social Security numbers are highly sensitive personal data that should only be shared with trusted persons in secure transactions.

purposes. Children receive Social Security numbers so that parents can claim them as dependents on their tax forms.

Social Security numbers are used as a primary identification tool for a variety of purposes. The numbers can be found on employment documents, Social Security Administration statements, credit applications, medical records, and some direct-deposit pay stubs. A thief who knows where to look can easily obtain someone's Social Security number. Once a thief has that number, he or she can do almost anything with it—apply for credit, get a job, open a bank account, and file tax information. Often agencies do not match Social Security numbers with birth dates to verify identities.

Just because someone asks you for your Social Security number does not mean you have to provide it. There are only two reasons to give out your Social Security number: to an employer (who needs the number for tax purposes) and to financial institutions, such as credit card companies and banks. If others ask for it, you should always ask why the information is needed and how the number will be used.

Never carry a Social Security card in a wallet or purse. It should be kept in a safe (preferably locked) location at home.

Personal Identification Numbers

Personal identification numbers (PINs) are most often used at automated teller machines (ATMs). A person swipes a debit or credit card and then is asked to punch in a PIN on a keypad. Thieves obtain PINs in many ways. In some cases, they are easily stolen along with a card because people have written them down instead of memorizing them. At other times, thieves sit in a strategic location from which they can watch an ATM, or they may set up a camera near or on an ATM to capture information. If a thief with a stolen card also knows the PIN, he or she can withdraw money from a victim's account.

Driver's License Numbers

Driver's licenses are often used as a primary method of identification. They not only give someone the legal right to drive a car but also verify a person's identity when cashing checks, voting, and boarding commercial airline flights. All a thief needs to make a phony driver's license is a driver's license number. Sophisticated technology allows thieves to create documents such as driver's licenses that appear authentic. A criminal can take a driver's license number and make a new license with his or her own picture on it. That's all it takes to start living a life as someone else.

Passwords

Many people have dozens of passwords for different online accounts and websites. People pay bills, do their banking, and order merchandise online. Each online account requires a password. Once a thief has a user name and password, he or she can unlock all types of information associated with an account. He can start buying merchandise in someone else's name or hijack valuable financial data.

Identity thieves can sometimes guess passwords, especially if people have incorporated birth dates, children's names, or pets' names. Passwords are tougher to crack when they include an apparently random combination of letters, numbers, and special

Identity Theft Reports by State

In 2017, personal finance website WalletHub conducted an analysis to determine in which states Americans are most and least vulnerable to identity theft. It combined eight metrics, taking into account not only the number of complaints and average loss due to fraud, but also what policies were in place to protect consumers. California was ranked the worst state for identity theft offenses, with Connecticut, Rhode Island, Illinois, and New York filling out the top five. South Dakota was the state in which people were reportedly safest from identity theft.

It is hard to know exactly why one state or city has a high number of complaints. Does more identity theft happen in those places, or are people simply more willing to report it? Experts have their theories. For instance, large population centers are attractive to criminals such as pickpockets, who can find plenty of opportunities to steal wallets and purses that may hold important financial information.

An increase in identity theft in certain areas can also be attributed to a larger elderly population, which can be more vulnerable to this type of crime. Florida, ranked the fourth-worst state for identity theft, is home to many "snowbirds," retirees who move somewhere warm for the winter. More elderly people are also choosing to live year-round in this state, both in their own homes and in assisted-living facilities or nursing homes. Yet Arizona, another snowbird state, was ranked thirtieth on the list of worst states for identity theft, so it's hard to know whether this theory holds water.

There is a correlation with illegal drugs, too. Places that see a lot of drug activity often find higher reports of identity theft. The two crimes can go hand-in-hand, as drug users pilfer others' identities as a way to support their habits.

characters (such as #, $, or %). It is also recommended that individuals avoid using the same password for multiple accounts, and that online passwords be changed on a regular basis.

Card Transactions

Unscrupulous servers or employees at restaurants and businesses with access to customer credit cards can easily jot down account numbers. Technological advances have made this type of crime easier than ever. A handheld device called a skimmer can swipe dozens of credit cards and store the information. Other devices are installed at ATMs in order to record your PIN with keypad overlays, read your card's magnetic strip, or even take photos of your card.

Skimming can be hard to track or identify. Look out for ATMs and card readers at gas pumps whose components have become loose or partially dislodged; these may have skimmers installed. Ensure that restaurant and business employees don't keep your card out of your sight too long and check your account regularly for fraudulent charges.

Victims of Identity Theft

Victims pay the price in numerous ways: ruined credit, resulting in the inability to obtain loans for cars and homes; hours spent trying to rectify the situation; even criminal investigations in which they are the target. Targeted consumers often spend hours and hundreds of dollars to resolve the damage to their name and credit. A survey conducted by the Identity Theft Research Center (ITRC) in 2016 found that 26 percent of victims had to borrow money from friends and family, and 15 percent had to sell their possessions, relocate, or even move. Many identity theft victims say they have had problems getting credit or finding a job after the theft. Some have even been the targets of criminal

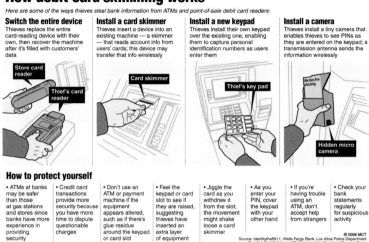

How debit card skimming works

Here are some of the ways thieves steal bank information from ATMs and point-of-sale debit card readers:

Switch the entire device
Thieves replace the entire card-reading device with their own, then recover the machine after it's filled with customers' data

Store card reader

Thief's card reader

Install a card skimmer
Thieves insert a device into an existing machine — a skimmer — that reads account info from users' cards; this device may transfer that info wirelessly

Card skimmer

Install a new keypad
Thieves install their own keypad over the existing one, enabling them to capture personal identification numbers as users enter them

Thief's key pad

Install a camera
Thieves install a tiny camera that enables thieves to see PINs as they are entered on the keypad; a transmission antenna sends the information wirelessly

Hidden micro camera

How to protect yourself

• ATMs at banks may be safer than those at gas stations and stores since banks have more experience in providing security	• Credit card transactions provide more security because you have more time to dispute questionable charges	• Don't use an ATM or payment machine if the equipment appears altered, such as if there's glue residue around the keypad or card slot	• Feel the keypad or card slot to see if they are raised, suggesting thieves have inserted an extra layer of equipment	• Jiggle the card as you withdraw it from the slot; the movement might shake loose a card skimmer	• As you enter your PIN, cover the keypad with your other hand	• If you're having trouble using an ATM, don't accept help from strangers	• Check your bank statements regularly for suspicious activity

© 2008 MCT

Source: Identitytheft911, Wells Fargo Bank, Los Altos Police Department
Graphic: Karl Kahler and Rob Hernandez, San Jose Mercury News

It is important to learn to recognize when a card skimmer has been installed on an ATM. This way, you can ensure that your debit card information is not stolen.

investigations and have been arrested for crimes committed by others in their names.

The emotional and personal costs can be devastating. According to a 2017 survey, 75 percent of victims were severely distressed by the theft, 66 percent felt violated, and 56 percent experienced rage or anger. In fact, one in four sought professional help to deal with these emotions. It's not hard to understand why the emotional toll is so great: identity theft impacts victims' personal and professional lives in big ways. Almost one in three had to reallocate time that they would have dedicated to life experiences such as vacations or hobbies in order to resolve the problem, with 22 percent having to spend time away from family or take time off work. Many reported that their relationships with family and friends had been negatively impacted by the theft.

Chapter Two

KINDS OF IDENTITY THEFT

Thieves have invented a slew of different ways to steal from and impersonate their victims. They will sometimes target specialized groups, such as members of the military. They will also seek to redirect essential benefits, such as disaster relief, into their own pockets. Some types of identity crimes have been around for many years, while others are fairly new. Law enforcement officials are left guessing what new types might emerge in coming years.

Financial Identity Theft

One of the most common forms of identity theft is financial identity theft, in which a criminal uses

Opposite: Identity thieves seek out their victims' personal information from a variety of sources, including medical forms and online sources, in order to perpetrate their crime.

someone else's personal information either to access an existing account or to open a new account in the victim's name. In the case of the former, known as "account takeover," thieves will either add their addresses to existing accounts or put themselves on the account as an authorized user. When thieves use information to open new accounts, they often do so to obtain cell phones or credit cards. Account takeover crimes tripled between 2016 and 2017, with total losses reaching $5.1 million, according to one study.

Criminals who gain access to credit card information use it to create counterfeit cards, which they can then use to make purchases. In 2015, however, cards with microchips that made them more difficult to counterfeit were introduced in the United States. The initiative worked: Visa reported that counterfeit fraud was down 52 percent at stores that could scan microchips. However, in response, criminals shifted to a new strategy in 2016, focusing instead on opening new accounts and making online purchases. Fraud committed when a card wasn't present for the transaction (as is the case with online purchases) increased 40 percent that year.

Medical Identity Theft

Given rising health-care costs in the United States, it is not surprising that one of the emerging and fast-growing categories of identity theft involves obtaining someone else's personal information for medical purposes. A simple visit to a doctor can cost hundreds of dollars, with medical procedures running into the thousands. Out-of-pocket costs for prescription drugs can be hundreds or thousands of dollars a month. Health expenditures in the United States number into the trillions of dollars.

The Ponemon Institute reports such theft is growing by 15 percent a year, with 2.3 million adults victimized annually. Victims face particularly high costs, with 29 percent incurring personal costs

of more than $5,000. For 86 percent of victims, it took more than six months to resolve their problem—an inordinately long time compared to the average identity theft.

Medical identity theft can be separated into three categories. One type of thief uses personal information to obtain health services by using the identity—and health coverage—of an insured person. Monthly health insurance premiums can be expensive if a person does not have coverage through an employer, and this type of thief may feel desperate for medical care. In the second category, medical facility personnel may be involved in an identity theft crime ring. They abuse their privacy privileges to get patient's health insurance information, and then either use it to submit false bills to the insurance company or sell the health policy information to others. The third group consists of people who use others' health coverage to buy prescription drugs. These people may have a prescription drug habit themselves or may sell the drugs on the street.

Medical information is supposed to be tightly guarded. The Health Insurance Portability and Accountability Act (HIPAA) of 1996 governs who can and who cannot access someone's private medical information. In theory, individuals' private medical records are closely protected. However, HIPAA security rules can be breached. Unethical employees who have access to information can give it or sell it to anyone. Breaches of HIPAA can also happen accidentally. A stack of papers on a busy receptionist's desk can fall into the wrong hands if no one is watching.

Targeting Members of the Military

As cruel as it sounds, identity thieves sometimes exploit the unique situation of military personnel to commit their crimes. In 2013, the FTC reported that military members experienced identity theft twice as often as the general public. Many service members don't have the time to keep a close eye on their credit reports or other financial statements, especially if they are deployed. If an identity thief accesses accounts or other information from a member of the military, it may be several months before the thief is caught. Resolving identity-theft issues can compound the stress of military life.

The US Department of Defense is taking steps to reduce the instances of identity theft among military personnel. For years, the military has relied solely on Social Security numbers as identifiers. However, more recently, identification cards instead use a bar code or magnetic strips that contain information. The Department of Defense also educates personnel on identity theft issues and trains those in charge of data in practices that keep it safe. Meanwhile, service members are reminded that it is illegal for anyone to make copies of their military ID, even though some businesses may attempt to do so.

Service members on active duty can request an "active duty alert" upon a credit report. A call to just one of the three major credit-reporting agencies is all it takes to get the alert placed on all three credit reports. This alert requires creditors to check with the account holder before issuing new lines of credit. The alert lasts for one year, but it can be lifted before that time or extended with a phone call. In addition, the account holder can designate someone to act as his or her representative during deployment.

More and more medical records are going online or are stored in computer databases, but this does not necessarily mean medical information will be more closely guarded. By 2016, 95 percent of US hospitals were effectively using health information technology and participating in the Centers for Medicare and Medicaid Services' Electronic Health Record Incentive Programs. These programs, established in 2011, encourage medical institutions to electronically capture clinical data and make it electronically available to patients.

However, this convenience may come at a price. Identity thieves can of course access paper records, but enterprising criminals can also hack into a database and—in just a matter of seconds—acquire information on hundreds or even thousands of people. Facilities generally encrypt data, but that does not make it immune to attack.

In recent years, more medical facilities have hired data integrity specialists tasked with carefully assessing how private medical information is stored and who has access to it. This oversight can help reduce instances of medical identity theft. Facilities that properly manage the disposal of information (purging outdated records from computers and shredding paper documents) lessen the risk of information falling into the wrong hands.

Medical facilities have to be careful about what type of access to patient information new employees can have. A system in which one person is responsible for the entire billing process is a system that is vulnerable to fraud because no one is watching over that person's shoulder. A system of checks and balances in which many people oversee each other's work is a safer, more private system.

Trying to correct medical identity fraud can be as time-consuming as correcting financial fraud. Victims of medical identity theft often do not know that their insurance information has been stolen until they get bills for medical care they never received. Then they have to prove to the health insurer that their identity was used by someone else, correct their medical records, and sort through what can be damaging false information about their medical histories. They may find it difficult to obtain their rightful benefits or continue their health insurance coverage. It can take months or even years to clear false information.

Immigration Identity Theft

Identities can be stolen by people who want to work under a different name. Some people who come to the United States without proper documentation have used alternative identities to secure employment. Often, the Social Security number of a US citizen is all someone needs to get a job and assume that citizen's identity in the workplace. A US Treasury Inspector General for Tax Administration audit released in 2017 reported that approximately 1.4 million undocumented immigrants used stolen or falsified Social Security numbers in 2015 to get a job.

The identity of a real person must be used in obtaining a job because many employers do background checks on employees. A background check investigates only the name and Social Security number provided; it does not verify that employees are who they say they are. An identity thief can work indefinitely as someone else as long as he or she is not caught. The Social Security Administration verifies that the number is real, but it does not check to see how many times that number is being used. One Social Security number could be used many times by many different people. In Ottawa, Kansas, for example, one woman was surprised to get a letter from the Internal Revenue Service (IRS) asking for $3,300 in unpaid taxes. The taxes were related to five different jobs in several different states in which the woman had never worked. It turns out that her identity had been used by undocumented immigrants.

The Theo Lacy Facility in Orange, California, houses criminals and immigration detainees. Some immigrants use stolen Social Security numbers in order to obtain a job.

US Immigration and Customs Enforcement (ICE) identifies benefit fraud as another high-priority offence committed by some immigrants. One example of this was the case of a Mexican man who, in 1980, acquired a false birth certificate and ultimately obtained a Social Security number, US passport, and driver's license. For the next thirty-seven years, he lived in Tijuana, Mexico, but collected $361,000 in US government benefits.

Uncovering immigration-related identity theft is difficult. Employers can face legal trouble if they are discovered to have hired undocumented immigrants. However, many argue that there is not much they can do to find out if their potential employees are using false names. Federal antidiscrimination laws prohibit employers from asking too many questions of applicants. That means they often have to believe that the documents they are given are real. Even if employers doubt a person is who he says he is, the law might prohibit them from inquiring further.

Those familiar with identity theft say there are many flaws in the system that allow this type of identity theft to occur. For example, the IRS can determine through database records who is not paying taxes, but it cannot determine who is using false identification. Even if officials suspect that a Social Security number is being used improperly, investigating identity theft is not one of the IRS's responsibilities.

Some blame US immigration policy as a whole. Critics say current policy makes it difficult for immigrants to come here legally. In Mexico, immigrants who want to come to the United States legally sometimes must wait seven or more years. Those looking for the chance to make money may not feel that they can wait. As a result, they come to the United States without the proper documentation.

Perhaps another solution to this problem is to issue driver's licenses and other governmental documents to undocumented immigrants. Cities such as San Francisco, California, and New Haven, Connecticut, give official ID cards to undocumented immigrants. In this way, the identity of the cardholder is verified. This reduces the need for someone to fake an identity to work or open bank accounts. However, critics of this plan say that it is dangerous to give undocumented immigrants official, government-issued documents and that doing so raises security concerns in an age marked by terrorism.

To what extent identity theft should be prosecuted in undocumented immigration cases recently went all the way to the US Supreme Court. Since 2004, federal prosecutors had been able to extend sentences of undocumented immigrants if they were found to knowingly be using Social Security numbers belonging other people. This approach was used in one of the biggest immigration raids in US history. In the summer of 2008, nearly four hundred immigrants were arrested at a plant in Postville, Iowa. Of that number, 270 were charged with identity theft. Most of the latter group served their sentences and were deported. However, in May 2009, the Supreme Court justices ruled unanimously that government prosecutors went too far in using identity theft laws to lengthen the jail terms of undocumented workers.

In many cases, undocumented immigrants do not know they are using the Social Security number of an actual person. A randomly generated nine-digit number may—or may not—

result in a number that matches another person's Social Security number. The Supreme Court justices said that prosecution using the federal identity theft law relied too much on chance. That is, if the random Social Security number was actually the real number of another person, two more years would be added to an illegal immigrant's prison sentence. However, if the random number did not happen to match a real number, then the immigrant would be spared additional prison time.

Critics say that immigrants who use different identities to get jobs should not be prosecuted in the same way as other identity thieves. Some define identity theft as using another person's information in order to steal or profit. They argue that illegal immigrants are using information to find work, not gain possessions, and therefore should be treated differently.

Immigrants, too, can be at risk of identity theft. In 2018, a lawyer for the ICE field office in Seattle, Washington, was charged with one count of aggravated identity theft for allegedly attempting to steal the identities of seven individuals undergoing immigration proceedings.

Obtaining Disaster Benefits

When disaster strikes, identity thieves see an opportunity. Governments provide assistance for victims of natural disasters, such as floods, tornadoes, and hurricanes. Such assistance includes money for shelter, food, or other necessities.

In the aftermath of Hurricane Katrina in August 2005, many thieves helped themselves to the identities of disaster benefits recipients in Louisiana and Mississippi. The hurricane displaced many people from their homes in New Orleans and other nearby areas along the Gulf Coast. Residents had quickly evacuated the region prior to the hurricane, leaving important belongings behind. In the days after the storm, while law enforcement officials were busy keeping people safe, thieves had nearly unlimited access to paperwork and other documents that had not been secured.

Almost immediately, the government realized the high possibility of fraud and created the Hurricane Katrina Fraud Task Force in September 2005 to deter thieves and investigate fraud complaints. Even years after Hurricane Katrina, victims were still finding that their personal information had been leaked. For example, in late 2008, the Federal Emergency Management Agency (FEMA) reported that nearly seventeen thousand names, Social Security numbers, and telephone numbers of Katrina victims had been posted to two public websites. The information was removed as soon as FEMA officials discovered it. Also in 2008, a government subcontractor sent letters with personal information in mistakenly addressed envelopes. This mistake affected about a thousand people. In that case, FEMA offered identity theft monitoring to all those affected. In response to all the fraud around Katrina, the Department of Justice established the National Center for Disaster Fraud, which now receives hundreds of calls per month.

Today, new scams and frauds pop up after every large disaster. Some people have had their identity stolen by FEMA impersonators. In other cases, thieves set up websites claiming to collect funds for disaster relief, only to keep the money for themselves. Robocalls warn people that their flood insurance is past due and urge them to send money at once.

To keep from falling prey to such scams, people in disaster-prone areas are urged to keep important personal documents in a locked box. Copies should be stored together so they're easy to grab in case of emergency or evacuation. During the chaos in the wake of a disaster, victims often need official documents to jump-start the insurance claim and benefits process. Victims who are carrying personal documents with them should keep track of them at all times. An identity thief may be lurking anywhere and often will strike when people are at their most vulnerable.

Funding Terrorist Activities

A big concern in the aftermath of the September 11, 2001, attacks is people using false names to perpetrate criminal activity that results in terrorism.

Hurricane Katrina and subsequent flooding devastated New Orleans—and put identity information at risk.

Six of the nineteen terrorists involved in those attacks were using false Saudi Arabian passports and names.

What may seem like an ordinary criminal identity theft case may actually lead federal investigators to terrorist cells. Terrorists have used identity theft to obtain employment in someone else's name and to gain access to secure areas. An al-Qaeda terrorist cell in Spain used stolen credit cards to make purchases needed for terrorist activities. The stolen credit cards, along with stolen telephone cards, were used to communicate with other members of the organization in the Middle East. False passports and other travel documents were used to open bank accounts that supported terrorist activities.

Likewise, in 2017, fourteen people were convicted by a Belgian court of falsifying identity documents. Some of these documents had been sold to militants allegedly involved in terror attacks in Paris in November 2015 and Brussels in March 2016.

Chapter Three

HOW IDENTITY THEFT IS PERPETRATED

Whether they're tricking people into sharing personal information, stealing credit card numbers, or breaching big companies' databases, identity thieves are always developing new ways to circumvent security measures and get what they want. Some methods are used again and again, simply because they work. Others employ new technologies or strategies. However, the more potential victims become aware of the ways in which identity thieves commit their crimes, the more likely identity theft can be slowed or even stopped.

Common Scams

Identity thieves will often trick people into revealing personal information. These thieves do not need to

Opposite: One of the classic methods of identity theft is seeking out personal information via false invoices sent by mail.

steal wallets or purses. They simply persuade victims to give out account information, birth dates, and the like. They rely upon several tried-and-true scams to obtain identities and then start committing fraud and other crimes.

Online Fraud and Synthetic Identity Theft

Just as the internet has made it easier for thieves to use others' personal information to make purchases, it has also facilitated their direct access to bank and credit card accounts, since all the information associated with such accounts is available over the web. When thieves take control of accounts, they often change the password, gaining complete control over the victim's money or credit. They may even ransom the account, demanding that the owner pay a specified amount of money in exchange for relinquishing control. By 2018, online credit fraud was 81 percent more likely than theft occurring at the point of sale, such as at a cash register.

Stolen payment or account information can be used to purchase items online and ship those items to the thief's address. After new cards with hard-to-counterfeit microchips were introduced in the United States in 2015, online fraud increased, because buyers do not need to use a physical card in order to make a transaction. Experian reported that e-commerce fraud was up more than 30 percent in the first six months of 2017.

Meanwhile, Experian reported in 2018 that synthetic identity theft represented 80 to 85 percent of all identity fraud, making it the fastest-growing kind. Thieves merge consumer data such as Social Security numbers and addresses, often bought on the dark web, to create entirely new identities. This type of theft is difficult to prevent because it is still new, but as of 2017, financial institutions were creating advanced prevention methods.

Helpful Hint: Individuals should research tools that will help them monitor the dark web for elements of their identity.

The Phony Bank Examiner

This scam operates over the telephone. Someone calls and says he or she is an official at the bank where the victim has an account. The caller says there has been a problem at the bank and asks the victim to verify information such as account numbers, recent activity, or balances. The caller also tries to determine whether the person lives alone or is otherwise vulnerable to a scam. He or she says another bank official will be in touch with more information.

Sometime later that day, the victim will get another call. This one is from a person claiming to be a bank examiner. The bank examiner says that a dishonest teller is stealing money. The victim is asked to withdraw a large sum of money and deposit it into another account in hopes of catching the fictitious teller. The victim is told that the money is fully insured and that nothing will happen to it, but in reality, the account is set up in the thief's name. Sometimes the callers even go so far as to meet with the victims and produce phony receipts that show the transactions.

Helpful Hint: Anyone claiming to be a bank official should show proof of identity. In a situation like this, it is best to call the bank (not simply let them call you) to find out if indeed there are any problems.

Rigged ATMs

ATMs allow quick and convenient access to cash anywhere, anytime. People do not hesitate to swipe a card and punch a few keys in order for the machine to spit out money. But anywhere there is money, there are thieves hoping to profit.

Thieves use a variety of methods to steal information from ATMs. For example, they can attach wireless devices that are engineered to gather card numbers and PIN information. The devices mimic real ATM card slots. They are hard to detect,

Some ATMs can be rigged with wireless card slots, false keypads, and even tiny cameras in an attempt to steal personal information.

and most people cannot tell that they are not using a legitimate ATM. Thieves may be waiting nearby as their device reads the account numbers wirelessly. They also can aim a tiny camera at the keypad in order to capture PIN numbers.

Another way to steal PINs is to place a thin keypad over the original keypad. This way, thieves can record the numbers that victims punch in. Again, this phony keypad can be hard for the average person to detect.

Identity thieves will generally rig several ATMs in one area. They most often strike during weekends and holidays for two reasons: one, the ATMs are busier because people generally withdraw more cash during these times and two, many banks are closed and thieves can swipe a large amount of money before the victims can notify their banks and close an account.

The Census Count and Identity Theft

With increased awareness of identity theft, the good news is that more people are wary about sharing personal information. This posed a problem, however, for 2010 US Census Bureau workers, who in early 2009 were canvassing neighborhoods to verify addresses. Many workers reported that people were less willing to give out information, even when it was just an address. This wariness was understandable, because identity thieves have been known to pose as census workers to obtain Social Security numbers and other sensitive data.

Some identity thieves may pose as census workers, so never give out sensitive data.

In 2015, with the American Community Survey underway, threats did indeed pop up. A Missouri couple received a mailing that asked them to fill out an online survey, but they grew suspicious when some of the questions asked them when they leave for work and how much money was in their bank account. Thieves routinely pretend to represent Medicare, the Internal Revenue Service, law enforcement personnel, and other government agencies in order to obtain personal information.

Legitimate US census and other government workers never ask for Social Security numbers, donations, your mother's maiden name, or bank or credit card account numbers. Census workers can be identified by their badges, and they often carry handheld computers with them. If asked, they will provide the phone number of a supervisor. Real US census workers take an oath not to reveal personal data to anyone. Violation of that oath can result in a $250,000 fine or five years in jail.

Helpful Hint: Be aware of any ATM that looks unusual. The card slot may be cracked, or the screen may display odd instructions. Always shield the keypad with your hand in case a small camera is mounted somewhere nearby. Try to use ATMs that are operated by a bank instead of a private individual or company.

Card Verification

This is another scam done over the telephone. Callers use many scenarios to try to get victims to reveal credit card information. For example, a caller might say he is investigating fraudulent charges on behalf of a credit card company, and he needs a credit card number and expiration date to aid in the investigation. Or a caller may pose as an online merchant and say she needs to verify card information for payment. Once a thief has a card number, an expiration date, and the smaller verification number (called the Card Verification Code, or CVC) on the back, he or she can start racking up charges.

Helpful Hint: Never give out credit card information when prompted by a caller. The only time people should reveal account information over the phone or online is when they have initiated the contact.

Lottery Claims

Some victims receive a call, letter, or email that says they have won a lottery in a foreign country. The scammer claims that before the payment can be processed, officials need personal information such as full name, date of birth, telephone number, and a account number at a bank to which the money can (supposedly) be transferred.

Helpful Hint: Disregard any notices that claim lottery winnings. In order to win a lottery, people have to buy a ticket or register for a drawing. People are not randomly chosen to win money.

False Charities

It is human nature to want to help those who are less fortunate. Unfortunately, identity thieves take advantage of this compassion by soliciting money for phony charities. A caller will claim she works for a charity that is looking for donations, then ask for a credit card number and expiration date. Because so many legitimate charities ask for donations by phone, it can be difficult to distinguish what is real from what is not.

Thieves even use particular tragedies in order to prey upon people at their most generous. After the 9/11 terrorist attacks, many victims were duped into providing personal information by hustlers who called and requested money for a 9/11 victims' fund that did not exist.

Charity-related theft doesn't just occur over the phone. If you donate furniture, remember to empty the drawers; for clothing, empty the pockets; and for technology such as computers, look up the proper way to thoroughly and completely wipe the hard drive. In one case, a woman visiting a Goodwill store was able to buy thirty-nine pounds of personal documents, including medical records, insurance information, and checking account information.

Helpful Hint: Before donating money through an unsolicited request, take time to check out the charity. Most states require that charities register with the attorney general's office. A legitimate charity will have a way to donate securely over the internet, and its website will have easy-to-find phone numbers and emails of staff members who can respond to inquiries. Another way to confirm that a charity is legitimate is by checking the Better

Business Bureau's website, which grades charities' accountability based on a set of twenty standards.

Fake Invoices

In this scam, victims receive counterfeit (but authentic-looking) invoices either through the regular mail or through email. The invoice states that the victim bought something, and that now the payment is due. Elderly people can be especially vulnerable to this scam because they may think that they have forgotten to pay for an item. Thieves use the invoice to try to get victims to pay with a credit card or check, the account numbers of which will subsequently be stolen.

Helpful Hint: These invoices usually do not include a telephone number. Real businesses always include a telephone number and other contact information. When there is a phone number included on an invoice, people should always call to verify the invoice before sending money.

Temporary Account Suspension

In the case of this scam, victims receive a phone call or email that says an account has been suspended. The thief says that the bank is reviewing all accounts to check for fraud, and the victim must provide account information in order for the review to take place. Victims are asked for names, birth dates, account numbers, and PINs. If the information is not provided, victims are told, their account will be canceled.

Helpful Hint: Again, do not provide financial and personal information that is solicited from a stranger. A bank would never close someone's account because he or she failed to provide personal information.

Money Mule Schemes

Some people may be vulnerable to offers of easy and quick employment. A money mule scheme falls into this category. A person—called the "mule" (also a name for a person who transports drugs)—may get an offer via phone, email, or a website for a job as a financial manager or payment processor. A money mule is asked to open an account into which sums of money will be deposited. The person with the account is told he or she can keep a certain percentage, such as 10 percent. The person must forward the rest of the money to a different account.

What is really happening is that the money involved has been stolen, often through identity theft. The "employer" wants the money to come through an innocent account so it cannot be tracked. This is an illegal act of money laundering, and the "employee" is participating in the crime. What's more, the employee is likely to be the employer's next identity theft victim, having provided account information and perhaps other personal information.

Helpful Hint: Never agree to hold or transfer money for anyone else, especially for someone you don't know.

False Voting Registries

It happens every election year: criminals go door-to-door or contact victims over the phone, claiming that they work for an organization that registers people to vote. They ask for full Social Security numbers in order to complete the phony registration. In this way, they are able to obtain personal information from many people in a short amount of time.

Helpful Hint: Always ask for the organization's main phone number so you can call to verify the identities of people asking

Beware of false voting registries, in which a person or organization seeks personal information such as full Social Security numbers. Never share such information with someone you don't know.

for your information. If these people are working for a legitimate group, they will be happy to provide you with contact information.

High-Tech Dangers

While identity theft has always been a concern, there's no question that technology such as computers, online banking, and smartphones have made it easier than ever for thieves to steal personal information. Everyday habits on computers or mobile devices can result in identity theft. While people cannot be expected to unplug from these modern conveniences, there are ways to prevent identity theft when using technology. Consumers must first become aware of the dangers before they can take the proper precautions. The following are some high-tech traps thieves use to capture personal and financial information.

Malware and Spyware

An Ohio man was indicted in 2018 for allegedly hacking into thousands of computers, installing malware, and obtaining 24/7 surveillance of the individuals' computers. Such security breaches are quite common, and even a single attacker can perpetrate a massive theft.

Malware, a shortened term for malicious software, is any type of software designed to do damage to a computer or network. Spyware is a type of malware designed to spy on private information. Every day, people install programs that can—unbeknownst to them—look into their computer browsers, view the sites they are visiting, and extract personal information that is entered into those sites, such as names, addresses, and billing information. Spyware can be physically installed on a computer, or it can be remotely installed via the internet. Sometimes a victim has agreed to installing the remote spyware by clicking "I agree" on one of those long user agreements that are common during software installation. Few people read the fine print, which may actually reveal that the program is spyware.

File sharing also puts computers at risk for spyware monitoring. File sharing users agree to download software that connects their computers to a network of other users. This makes it easy to share games, music, and movies. However, it can also enable thieves to tap into a vast network of computers and install spyware that tracks personal information.

Besides simply looking for personal information, some spyware can monitor keystrokes. When a person types in a user name and password, those keystrokes are recorded. Keystroke spyware makes it easy for someone to obtain user names and passwords to get into otherwise-secure accounts.

Most often, these types of programs are unknowingly downloaded. Spyware lurks in email invitations and web advertisements.

Helpful Hint: Do not download even innocent-looking programs from unknown sources. Email attachments, links, and advertisements are common hiding places used by people trying to infect other computers with spyware. Even a harmless-looking program could contain spyware that results in identity theft. Install spyware protection software on your computer.

Wi-Fi Networks

These days, you can take a laptop computer almost anywhere and connect to the internet through wireless networks, often free of charge. Connecting to the wrong Wi-Fi network, however, can put your data at risk. In 2017, $117,000 in Bitcoin—a digital currency—was stolen from a man's account while he was connected to a restaurant's public Wi-Fi network in Austria. They were moved to an account that police found impossible to trace.

In wireless networks, information is sent over radio waves. Hackers can find ways to tap into unprotected wireless networks and intercept the information that is being sent. User names, passwords, and account information are vulnerable as a result. Wireless routers typically have a range of three hundred feet or more. That means a household's wireless network can be tapped into from a neighbor's house or from the street. It is not uncommon for thieves to drive through the streets with their laptops, checking for unsecured networks. Thieves can even set up their own wireless networks—often called "Free Wi-Fi" or something similar—in popular locations in order to lure people to connect.

Make sure that you only download files from trusted and secure web sources. Some downloads may hide malware, which can access personal information stored on your computer or online.

Network providers are coming up with better security options for customers. For example, Verizon allows wireless network users to install their own encryption if they are linked to an unencrypted network (which often happens in wireless "hot spots" or public places).

Helpful Hint: Make sure your computer or smartphone isn't set to automatically connect to any nearby Wi-Fi; instead, only use networks that are secure. Homes and businesses should always have password-protected wireless networks. If an unsecured network must be used, be sure not to visit websites that contain personal or financial information, such as the sites of banks or other financial institutions. Also ensure that any website you do visit has "https" in the URL; this will help to keep your information secure. Even better, connect via a Virtual Private Network (VPN) service, which encrypts your data for anyone trying to access it.

Phishing

Identity thieves often go "phishing" for information. This means that they troll the waters of the internet, hoping to lure someone into giving up personal information, such as user names, passwords, or account numbers.

In a typical example of phishing, a scammer will send a legitimate-looking email to an unsuspecting victim. The email claims to be from a bank, financial institution, or any company that holds account information. The email may claim that an account is out of date and that information needs to be re-entered or verified. Victims are told to either respond to the email or click on a link to a website and enter their information there. The phony website often looks so real that victims trust the request; some thieves even set up fake websites that look exactly like a real bank's site. Once victims enter their information, thieves have access to it. At any one time, there are millions of phishing sites in operation.

Banks are fighting phishing scams on their own terms. Most often, when a financial institution obtains knowledge of a phishing scam that directs customers to a phony website, officials will ask internet service providers to shut down the site. In October 2008, Bank of America began taking this one step further. Instead of simply shutting down the phishing site, the internet service provider was instructed to redirect people to an informational page created by the bank. This page told customers that they had been lured to a phony site by a phishing scam. It gave information on how to avoid this type of fraud in the future. Seven months after the program went into effect, more than seventy thousand people had been redirected to the educational page.

The number of phishing websites continues to increase. About 1.4 million phishing websites were created every month during the first half of 2017, according to a study by cybersecurity company Webroot. Most of the sites were online for only four to eight hours, making it more difficult for the crime to be discovered. Google was the most imitated site: 35 percent of all attempts at phishing tried to emulate this popular search engine. Other commonly imitated or impersonated companies were PayPal, Facebook, Dropbox, Chase, Yahoo, Apple, Wells Fargo, Adobe, and Citibank.

In recent years, banking regulators have required that institutions with online banking services take extra steps in guarding against phishing. Not only do customers log in with a user name and password, but an image chosen by the customer (such as a bird or television set) is also displayed on the screen. This image lets customers know that they are using the bank's authentic site, and not a "dummy" one. Other methods of two-factor authentication have been implemented, such as a means of verifying your identity by entering a code sent via text message to your phone.

Helpful Hint: Never enter personal information in any website that you have reached via a hyperlink in an email. If you want to access a bank or other online account, always type the URL directly into the search bar rather than following a link.

Tax Scams

Tax season is a busy time for identity thieves. Each spring, scammers send out emails that look as if they come from the IRS. The email may ask the recipient to supply personal information in order to receive a tax refund. The real IRS never initiates contact with taypayers via email, social media, or text message.

During tax season, some scammers send out emails posing as the Internal Revenue Service, seeking out sensitive data.

Phishing schemes were listed on the IRS's "Dirty Dozen" list of tax scams in 2018. One of the latest techniques was stealing personal information from tax professionals, filing false returns, then direct-depositing funds into real bank accounts. Thieves would then impersonate the IRS or a collection agency in an attempt to regain the funds. The schemes could be quite elaborate, involving phone calls, websites, and emails.

During the first ten weeks of the 2017 tax season, another new scheme emerged: W-2 phishing scams tricked more than one hundred employers into handing over employees' personal information. Scammers often impersonated a CEO to send an email requesting employees' W-2 tax forms, which contain Social Security numbers and other important information.

Helpful Hint: Report tax-related attempts at identity fraud by emailing phishing@irs.gov.

Social Engineering

Some identity thieves need minimal information before striking. People may think they are safe from identity thieves because they do not share Social Security numbers or account information. However, these same people may not think twice about sharing other types of personal information. Savvy identity thieves use a tactic called social engineering to get people to reveal seemingly innocent information. Then they use these facts as the key to unlock more useful data.

For example, many people use a pet's name or a child's name as a password or PIN. Identity thieves with this information can try to hack into a person's account. In another form of social engineering, criminals approach banks and other institutions posing as actual customers. They try to get tellers and other employees to give out account information.

Helpful Hint: People should be very careful not to reveal too much personal information on social media. Banks and other financial institutions should always ask for verification of someone's identity before revealing account information or performing any transactions.

It may be difficult to believe how many people fall for some of these scams. Yet thieves steal millions of identities using these types of scams every year. Many thieves know how to make themselves sound official or produce official-looking documents. They prey on fear—fear that an account is closed, or fear that a teller is dishonest and will steal a victim's money. They also prey on peoples' desire for success or money by promising lottery winnings or other rewards. Just remember the old saying: if it seems too good to be true, it probably is.

Finally, when it comes to large data breaches, make sure to protect yourself by having a different password for every online account; if you don't, one hacked account can give thieves the key to access all your other accounts. Change your passwords regularly and stay abreast of data breach news. If a bank or other company with which you have an account is hacked, seek information on how to protect yourself immediately. It will likely be recommended that you change your username, password, or both.

Chapter Four

THIEVES AND HOW TO REPORT THEM

Who are identity thieves, and what motivates them? The possible answers to this question are in many senses as numerous as the number of thieves themselves. On the other hand, the underlying goal for any identity thief is simple: to achieve personal gain through the use of another person's identity. Understanding who they are and how they commit their crimes provides more insight into why it's sometimes difficult to find justice, and why some crimes are never reported at all.

Identity Thieves

Identity thieves are not always mysterious, shadowy criminals hiding behind computer screens. They can be relatives, friends, or next-door neighbors. They

Opposite: It can be hard to track down an identity thief, especially when they have perpetrated their attacks over the internet.

can be old or young. They can be the nicest person on the block. Most of all, they can be difficult to identify, in part because some of the rationalization behind their actions can be surprising.

The demand for cash to fuel an alcohol, drug, or gambling addiction can drive someone to use identity theft to obtain money in illegal ways. Addiction can cloud a person's judgment, causing even good people to act in ways that they otherwise wouldn't. Because an addict may already be used to breaking the law to obtain or pay for drugs, he or she may decide that there is no risk in compounding the problem.

Other identity thieves are particularly skilled at rationalizing their behavior. Rationalizing is an attempt to offer apparently logical reasons, even if these are not supported by actual fact. An identity thief may argue that he or she is using someone else's money to get out of serious trouble. It could be a single mother in danger of losing her home. It could be a son who needs to buy expensive medicine for a parent. They may feel they have nowhere else to turn, and that the ends justify the means.

Some thieves simply feel entitled to the money they have stolen. Evidence of living well is apparent in every aspect of today's society: luxury cars speed down roadways, grand houses pop up in new developments, and private schools offer exclusive educations to children. When people find themselves down on their luck, some may be willing to do almost anything to keep their lifestyles intact. The pressure to keep up with neighbors can also cause individuals to make poor choices.

Identity theft does not always result in financial fraud. Some people use a false identity to obtain work. They may be undocumented immigrants. Others might want to hide a checkered employment history. More employers today are requesting credit checks and refusing to hire people who have had financial problems. An employee may think that working under someone else's identity is the only way to get a job.

The majority of identity theft crimes are perpetrated by strangers, in which case victims may never find out who used their identities. Occasionally, however, friends and family members are the identity thieves, especially if the victim is a child or elderly person. People in desperate financial situations may seize the opportunity to obtain a friend or relative's personal information. Unfortunately, it is easy for identity thieves to abuse the trust common among friends and relatives. It is not difficult to slip a credit card from a wallet or take a blank check or a Social Security card when someone is not looking. Friends and relatives may be privy to personal information such as birth dates and maiden names that are used to verify accounts.

One thing is certain: an identity thief who turns out to be a friend or relative complicates the situation. There are many factors that victims need to take into consideration. How best to resolve the situation becomes a very personal decision.

Personally knowing the identity thief can make a difficult situation even harder. Many victims are reluctant to press charges or file a police report, especially if the thief is a close relative. Victims do not want to see their child or their mother thrown in jail. However, officials at the Identity Theft Resource Center point out that the victim is not responsible for the jail time or criminal charges; the thief brought it upon himself or herself by committing the crime.

Victims can make several choices when dealing with an identity thief they know. For one, they can treat this crime like any other and file a police report. Without a police report, it can be difficult to prove to creditors and credit bureaus that an identity theft has actually occurred.

A way to resolve the situation without criminal action is to hire a mediator. A mediator will help both victim and criminal reach an agreement on how outstanding bills can be paid. The agreement is legally binding.

The Emotional Impact of Identity Theft

Identity-theft victims often find themselves experiencing many different emotions as they try to resolve their cases. It is important to acknowledge the emotions and talk about them before they spiral out of control. Victims should speak to a trusted friend or relative about their situation and how they are addressing the problem. Other people can provide support and feedback during a victim's sensitive time.

When identity theft is first discovered, common emotions include surprise, embarrassment, anger, and the feeling of being alone. As they work to resolve the issue, victims may feel overwhelmed and frustrated. Resolving identity theft can require a great deal of paperwork, time, energy, and sometimes money. Phone calls and letters may go unanswered, and victims might be shuttled from one voicemail to another. It may seem like the problem will never end.

Then there is the feeling of insecurity and mistrust. It is hard to feel secure when someone has stolen personal information that is supposed to be confidential. If the thief was a relative or friend, it can be hard to develop trusting relationships again.

Those in charge of a household's finances may experience feelings of guilt and powerlessness. Identity theft can destroy credit ratings, making it difficult to purchase a house or a car. It can also completely change a family's routine and way of life. Achieving certain financial dreams may be delayed.

There are many ways to take control of the situation. Acknowledging the emotions is an important first step. Staying organized and on-task can help victims regain a sense of control. It is also important not to let

When a person's identity is stolen, they can suffer great emotional distress. Such theft leads victims to distrust others and experience high stress levels during the arduous process of repairing the damage.

the crime absorb all of one's time. Victims should take time to go out for dinner, catch a movie, or exercise. Some even find purpose in becoming advocates for identity theft awareness. They may join support groups or advocate for laws that assist victims or protect potential victims.

If the problem still seems overwhelming, it might be time to speak with a professional counselor, especially one who specializes in treating crime victims.

If victims are reluctant to file charges against a relative or friend, they can contact creditors to see if the situation can be resolved without police involvement. This usually demands the cooperation of both victim and criminal. Sometimes a creditor can be persuaded to transfer the bill to the identity thief. This will require a statement signed by the thief and sent to the creditor.

Some victims decide to do nothing and settle the debt themselves. Victims will sometimes choose this route if they want to protect the identity thief and give him or her another chance. In other cases, family members or other friends will pressure the victim into forgiving the situation. They may offer to help the victim pay off the debt, or they may work out a deal in which the thief agrees to pay off the debt. Victims should be aware that if they pay off the debt themselves, the poor credit reports and ratings will remain in their name. Choosing this route will not fix bad credit. Filing a police report is the only way to clear fraudulent credit records.

Famous Identity Theft Cases

It is no surprise that identity theft cases involving celebrities or outrageous actions can dominate national headlines.

One of the most famous identity theft cases involves a man named Frank Abagnale Jr. In the 1960s, Abagnale assumed a variety of identities, including that of an airline pilot and a doctor. He successfully forged payroll checks and stole more than $2 million through fraud. Abagnale primarily used check forgery as a means of stealing the identities of others, and he impersonated his victims as well. After the Federal Bureau of Investigation (FBI) caught up with Abagnale, he helped the agency find others who were also using identity theft scams. Abagnale's story was made into a critically acclaimed 2002 film, *Catch Me If You Can*, starring Leonardo DiCaprio as Abagnale

The 2002 film *Catch Me If You Can* is based on the life of Frank Abagnale Jr., who stole more than $2 million and took on a number of identities during the 1960s. Today, Abagnale works with the FBI.

and Tom Hanks as an FBI agent. Today, Abagnale continues to work with the FBI in identifying fraud cases and speaks to businesses and organizations around the country on topics related to fraud. According to his website, he does not accept payment for any of his work with the government; instead, most of his income is derived from public speaking and consulting for such large corporations as Experian and Intuit.

In another case, in New York City in 2001, Abraham Abdallah was charged with criminal impersonation, forgery, and fraud for allegedly using the personal information of celebrities and other wealthy individuals. Court documents say that Abdallah, a restaurant busboy, used a copy of *Forbes* magazine, the internet, and cell phones to obtain Social Security numbers, credit-card numbers, and financial records. When he tried to transfer $10 million from a top executive's brokerage account, company officials became suspicious and authorities were alerted. Authorities think that Abdallah may have obtained the personal information of such celebrities as Steven Spielberg, Oprah Winfrey, and Martha Stewart.

In the early 1990s, a man named James Rinaldo Jackson managed to compile personal information of dozens of Hollywood stars and Wall Street bankers. Perhaps most shocking, he was able to compile this information using a phone from inside a prison. All it took was one leak to open the door for Jackson. He started by finding out the name of the medical provider to the Screen Actors Guild. Then he called the provider and, pretending to be an administrator looking to verify medical bills, received the Social Security number, address, and date of birth for film director Steven Spielberg. He acquired Spielberg's credit-card records. He also accessed the personal and financial information of actors Mel Gibson and Danny DeVito. Accomplices helped him cover up his frequent phone calls from the prison phone, but he was eventually caught. Jackson, like Abagnale, later traveled the world, giving talks on how people can avoid the same type of scams he perpetrated.

In April 2009, an actor on the television series *One Tree Hill*, Antwon Tanner, was charged with selling Social Security numbers and cards. US Immigration and Customs Enforcement (ICE) officials caught Tanner selling the numbers over the phone. An informant tipped off an undercover agent, who ended up buying sixteen Social Security numbers and three falsified cards for $10,000 from the actor. It was not clear how the numbers had been obtained or what the plan was for using them. In January 2010, Tanner pleaded guilty in a federal courtroom in Brooklyn. He was sentenced to three months in prison and five months of house arrest.

The Reporting Process

Documenting identity theft and clearing one's good name takes time, effort, and often money. Victims are urged to contact their credit card companies and banks to immediately notify them of fraud. Many also try to contact their local law enforcement agency to file an official report.

However, it is here that frustration can take hold. The Identity Theft Resource Center reports that some of the most frequent complaints from victims center on law enforcement's response to their issues. In 2015, 47 percent of victims who worked with a law enforcement agency reported a poor or terrible level of satisfaction. Just one in three called the experience good or excellent. Victims often feel that law enforcement officials do not regard identity theft as a serious enough crime to warrant staff time and investigation. Or, if law enforcement does respond, victims may think officers are not acting fast enough or doing enough to catch the criminals. The truth of the matter is that many identity thieves are never caught. By the time their crimes are detected, they may have moved on. Or perhaps they were using public computers to perpetrate their crimes and cannot be traced. In any case, though, victims want to feel as if law enforcement is helping them.

In a 2013 guide for attorneys assisting clients with identity theft, the FTC recommended the following steps for beginning to address a case: first, initiate a fraud alert on credit reports; next, review credit reports for evidence of any other identity theft; and third, cancel any compromised accounts. The FTC hosts a website, IdentityTheft.gov, where consumers can report identity theft and access a recovery plan. Most sources suggest notifying your bank and credit card accounts first, then reporting the theft to the FTC in this way.

In some cases, obtaining a police report can help victims pursue justice. However, it has sometimes proven difficult to acquire such a report, in part because of confusion over which agency or jurisdiction is responsible for recording such an offense. Organizations such as the International Association of Chiefs of Police (IACP) have attempted to change this and make it easier for victims to obtain police reports. The IACP collaborated with other groups to found Operation Stop IT!, which helps train law enforcement to both prevent identity theft and help victims. Still, such training hasn't reached all corners of the country, and in 2017, people were still encountering challenges when seeking reports and experiencing confusion when trying to determine the best process for fighting identity theft.

Sometimes, law enforcement agencies do not have the time to fully investigate or solve the crime. Many law enforcement agencies, especially at local levels, are short-staffed and devote their energy to violent crimes such as assault, kidnapping, and homicide. However, it benefits law enforcement agencies to follow up on all reports of identity theft because the investigation may uncover larger, more serious crimes. Thieves often use false identities to deal drugs, evade arrest, and commit fraud.

Because identity thieves often cross through different jurisdictions, it is important for law enforcement officials to track criminals on the move. Different agencies need ways to share identity theft cases with one another.

The Consumer Sentinel Network, operated by the FTC, gives law enforcement access to millions of consumer complaints related to identity theft and other scams. Law enforcement officials can use the database to look for connections among different cases. Such research may even lead to the discovery of larger identity theft crime rings. Meanwhile, the National Identity Theft Victims Assistance Network provides victim-assistance training for professionals and maintains a victim-assistance map where consumers can seek out help and insight on local laws on a state-by-state basis.

Of course, any time governmental agencies collect personal data, there is a risk of privacy invasion. Civil libertarians—people concerned about privacy rights—worry that information stored in a database could be used for the wrong purposes. Perhaps an innocent person's information ends up in the database, and as a result, he or she is targeted by police. Do the benefits outweigh the risks? For every one hundred identity thieves caught because of such a database, is it all right if one innocent person is mistakenly targeted?

Underreporting Identity Theft

There are many indications that identity theft is underreported, especially in the case of ransomware—software that blocks the use of a computer until money is paid—mostly because victims are either embarrassed or feel that law enforcement can't help. The FBI reported only $17.4 million losses to ransomware and online extortion in 2016, yet total losses may have been $1 billion—more than ten times that amount. In other cases, stolen mail is often not missed, and those whose government benefits were stolen sometimes never find out, so these events aren't reported, either.

So why are these crimes so underreported? For one thing, law enforcement personnel in some states do not even take identity theft reports—or if they do, they don't investigate the matter. Victims may feel that no one is willing to help them, so why should they even bother reporting it? It also can be difficult to determine which jurisdiction should handle the complaint. So much identity theft occurs across state lines. Does the victim's local police department have jurisdiction? Or should law enforcement officials where the criminal lives take charge? This type of confusion can inhibit victims from filing complaints.

Victims can also be deterred by the anonymity of the crime. By the time the crime is discovered, the thief may have moved on to someone else. He or she may have used a public computer to commit crimes, making it even more difficult and time-consuming to track. In some cases, finding the criminal can be impossible.

Finally, systems put in place for tracking particular types of crimes are often not specific enough in their classification to provide a clear and consistent picture of how often identity theft occurs. According to the FBI, "the number of identity theft victims and total losses are likely much higher than publicly-reported statistics. It is difficult to provide a precise assessment because different law enforcement agencies may classify identity theft crimes differently, and because identity theft can also involve credit card fraud, Internet fraud, or mail theft, among other crimes."

Whose Responsibility?

Unlike other crimes—in which law enforcement officials take on the burden of investigation—when identity theft occurs, the victims bear most of the responsibility for documenting it. Already stressed by the discovery of the crime, victims face the added ordeal of spending time, money, and other resources on trying to resolve their cases. Victims must often become their own advocates.

Certainly, local law enforcement still has a role to play. Filing official police reports can help a victim get compensated for their losses or properly report their fraud to their banks. On the federal level, several agencies perform identity theft investigations. All reports of identity theft should be logged with the FTC. The FBI partners with state and local law enforcement, along with other federal agencies, to investigate violations of the 1998 Identity Theft and Assumption Deterrence Act and the 2004 Identity Theft Penalty Enhancement Act. The Department of Justice prosecutes such cases. Still other agencies, such as the Consumer Financial Protection Bureau, have been involved in investigating data breach cases in which millions of identities have been compromised. Many have argued that new data breach legislation is necessary to protect consumers from this pattern of ever-larger breaches, but Congress has not passed a law on the matter as of this writing.

However, in many cases, the victims are in the best position to gather and present evidence. For instance, they have access to the documents that show the fraudulent charges. It becomes important that the victim takes an active role in investigating the fraud and assisting law enforcement officials whenever possible. So, while law enforcement personnel and federal agencies continue to seek a solution to jurisdictional questions and conflicts, the individual victim still seems to play perhaps the most important role of all in the investigation of identity theft.

Chapter Five

FIGHTING BACK

Individuals, businesses, and the government all have a role to play in reducing the risk of identity theft, though these roles shift as new types of theft emerge. Taking precautions to ensure that personal information isn't exposed at home, in public, or online is the first step to ensuring the safety of one's personal data. It is also worthwhile to familiarize oneself with the protection that banks, credit card companies, and other institutions offer individuals who are worried about identity theft.

Businesses are interested in protecting their customers, so they are taking steps to make databases more secure, but with every improvement they make, computer-savvy identity thieves work to discover new

Opposite: Businesses, governments, and individuals worldwide are collaborating to enact new protections against identity theft.

loopholes. Meanwhile, the government has put laws into place that both criminalize identity theft and make it easier for consumers to keep track of their credit and to report crimes. Yet some of these laws, especially when it comes to data-gathering and ease of understanding, are not without controversy.

Individuals

People can reduce their risk of being identity theft victims by staying alert, acting smart, and not divulging personal information. It is possible to stay safe at home, in public, and online. Smart practices can keep your identity safer.

At Home

Even though many identity thieves use the anonymity and ease of the internet to commit their crimes, plenty of criminals still go about things the old-fashioned way: by rifling through people's mail and trash.

If possible, use a locked mailbox, either at the curb or at a post office. Avoid placing outgoing mail in an unsecured curb mailbox. Instead, take it directly to a post office collection box. Retrieve mail as soon as possible. Avoid letting it sit in an unsecured mailbox for any length of time. Shred credit card offers or other such documents before placing them in the trash or recycling bin. When moving, fill out a change-of-address form well in advance of the move.

Keep track of what types of mail come weekly or monthly (for example, bills). That way, it is easier to see what mail may be missing and possibly stolen. Report missing mail right away to postal officials. Better yet, sign up to receive online statements and bills only, so that you no longer receive paper mail containing this sensitive information.

Shred anything that contains your name and address, including credit card offers and statements, utility bills, and expired credit cards or driver's licenses. Remember, thieves do not need much personal information to get started.

In 2017, a new law was passed prohibiting the federal government from including Social Security numbers on mailed documents. The Social Security Number Fraud Prevention Act required agencies to specify any circumstances that might require an exception to this rule. The result, however, should be a decreased risk to consumers.

In Public

People are vulnerable to identity theft in any public place. First, carry as little personal information as possible. Purses and wallets often hold a variety of credit cards and other information. People should ask themselves if they need all this documentation every time they leave the house. It is necessary to have five or six credit cards at all times? Is it better to leave your checkbook at home? It is best to downsize whenever possible and take along only the most necessary information. This may include a driver's license and just one credit card. Never take a Social Security card out of your house.

Be aware of your surroundings and nearby people. Shoulder surfing is a practice in which criminals look over someone's shoulder at ATMs, the grocery store, or any place where someone needs to punch in passwords or PINs. With today's technology, people do not even need to be nearby when shoulder surfing. A digital camera or other recording device can be used from many feet away or can be pre-installed on an ATM. Be aware of any suspicious people.

Be careful what information is shared in a cell-phone conversation. Some people tend to have very private conversations in very public places. If the conversation is private or includes

Wireless Identity Theft

In the past few years, thieves have discovered a different way to steal credit card information without ever touching your card, and a new industry has sprung up to protect cardholders from theft. But should you really be worried?

Some cards are equipped with a small chip enabled with radio frequency identification (RFID). The chips send out radio signals and make it possible for you to pay without ever bringing your card in contact with a card reader. It's convenient, but the problem is that you can't turn these radio signals on and off. That means that thieves can point a handheld RFID scanning device at your wallet, pocket, or purse, and walk away with your credit card number, and even your expiration date. It's a scary prospect.

Since RFID chips were introduced a decade ago, a whole industry has sprung up. Specially made wallets, purses, and protectors ensure that your card will be safe from scanning. However, most cards in the United States still don't even have RFID chips. In 2016, about 26 million cards with RFID chips were issued. That's just around 4.7 percent of all payment cards in the country. However, all newer US passports have RFID chips.

So how do you know if your card has an RFID chip? There will probably be a small symbol resembling radio waves somewhere on the card. If you do have a card or passport with an RFID chip, it may be worthwhile to buy a special wallet—or, on the cheaper side, simply wrap your card or passport in a thick sheet of aluminum foil.

Many are concerned that credit card information can be stolen wirelessly from cards equipped with RFID chips.

sensitive information, it is best to talk quietly in a private place to prevent a potential identity thief from eavesdropping.

Receipts from credit or debit card transactions are sometimes stuffed into a purse or wallet, or haphazardly tossed into the nearest trash bin. It is important to keep these receipts and check them against bank statements. A person who faithfully keeps track of all transactions is more likely to catch identity theft shortly after it happens, thereby minimizing the potential for the crime to spiral out of control.

Online and on the Phone

Never provide unsolicited financial information. In other words, if someone calls you and asks for sensitive information, do not give it out. Generally, it is all right to reveal such information if you have initiated the call.

A good option for online purchases is to use a prepaid debit card instead of a credit card. For each purchase made with a debit card, the amount is subtracted from a set amount. This is in contrast to a credit card, in which transactions are added to an account, sometimes up to thousands of dollars. The advantage of using a prepaid debit card is that if the number were stolen, a thief could make purchases only up to the amount on the card. With these prepaid cards, it is a good idea to keep the maximum limit low.

Another tool that can reduce risk of identity theft is eWallet software. This software can be loaded onto a computer or handheld device. It uses encryption technology to store passwords and account numbers. This prevents the need to memorize or write down passwords. It also makes it easy to manage a number of different passwords, helping people avoid the temptation to use the same password for multiple accounts.

If purchases must be made with a credit card, use only one credit card for all online transactions. This will make the transactions easier to track, and consumers can note suspicious activity right away. Many people also choose to use a site such as PayPal to make online purchases, since PayPal ensures the security of your card information even if you are purchasing from a site that you are not completely certain is safe. PayPal has millions of customers, and it benefits the company to keep financial data secure. Still, breaches can occur anywhere. People concerned about their information being online might feel safer using a prepaid card or eWallet software.

Computers should be set to run automatic updates, and the latest version of a browser should always be installed. This will ensure that encryption is up-to-date. Updates that provide additional security patches and other measures are routinely made available. Make sure that any e-retail sites you shop at use encryption technology. The business will usually note the use of such technology somewhere on the site. If the site uses encryption, some browsers will show a small "lock" symbol in the search bar to indicate this. Most merchants send consumers an email confirming a purchase. Double-check the email to make sure that everything is correct and save the email for your records.

Identity Theft Protection Services

The rise in identity theft crime reports has led to a fast-growing business sector: companies that offer identity theft protection services. While some products are legitimate and do help to reduce the risk of identity theft, as with any product, individuals must watch for scams and misleading or false claims.

Advertising tactics by these companies are often aggressive and thereby generate criticism and controversy. For example, one company claimed that if individuals use its protection service and still fall prey to identity theft, the company will cover expenses up to $1 million. However, in reality, those expenses were related only to settling identity theft matters, not to any losses incurred in the theft itself. One catchy jingle offering free credit reports does not reveal the fact that people have to pay for a service before the free report is delivered to them. Many people have complained to the FTC about signing up for what they thought were free credit reports, only to learn they had been charged.

What these companies generally do not advertise is that they provide services that consumers could do themselves for free. For example, consumers have the legal right to obtain one free credit report each year from all three credit-reporting agencies. Consumers can also place fraud alerts and freezes on their credit reports, again for free. However, keeping on top of one's credit takes time and energy. Some individuals would rather pay companies a fee in exchange for not having to do the work themselves, just as many people pay for the convenience of having someone else change the oil in their cars. Others are willing to pay for the peace of mind of knowing that someone is always monitoring their credit. Consumers who choose this route should carefully research each company and devise a list of questions to ask before signing up for any service.

The following is a list of some identity-theft protection services and tips on how to evaluate those services.

Credit Monitoring Services

Under the Fair and Accurate Credit Transactions Act of 2003 (FACTA), consumers can access one free credit report each year from each of the three major credit bureaus: Experian, TransUnion, and Equifax. (FACTA in an amendment to the Fair Credit Reporting Act, or FCRA, which we'll learn about later.) However, an identity thief can do a lot of damage in a year, so some people choose to get more updates. The three credit reporting agencies also offer more frequent monitoring for $13 to $15 per month. Alternatively, people can hire a company to monitor their reports. The fees and what these businesses provide vary widely. For example, many companies will monitor only one of the credit bureaus, not all three. The FTC recommends carefully reading through a service plan before enrolling. In addition, it is smart to check with a state's attorney general's office or Better Business Bureau to see if there are any complaints on file about the company.

Credit monitoring does not prevent identity theft. It alerts consumers only after identity theft has already occurred, and then only if there is unusual activity on one of your accounts—for instance, if one of your payments is late or if your credit history is checked by a company. The FTC points out that credit monitoring won't warn you if an identity thief uses your Social Security number or withdraws cash from your bank account.

You can always find plenty of advertisements for "free credit reports." However, the FTC cautions that there is only one authorized website to trust for the truly free credit report: www.annualcreditreport.com.

Identity Monitoring

Identity monitoring services can let you know when your personal information is being used in unusual ways—for instance, if a change-of-address form has been filled out on your behalf, if you have taken out any payday loans, or if your personal information has shown up on social media sites or on websites where thieves typically post stolen information.

If you choose to contract with an identity monitoring service, remember to first ask what databases and types of information the service monitors, and how often. Also be sure to have a clear understanding of how the company will use your information— remember, you would be handing over some sensitive personal details. However, the FTC warns that most of these services aren't equipped to monitor government benefits or tax fraud.

Identity Theft Insurance

Many identity theft protection services offer identity theft insurance to businesses and individuals. The insurance does not help a consumer avoid identity theft; instead, it covers the costs associated with straightening out an identity theft case. These costs can include telephone calls, copying expenses, mailing expenses, and sometimes legal bills. Insurance companies generally do not reimburse customers for the money that has actually been stolen by an identity thief or for any financial losses caused by the crime.

Insurance products purchased through reputable companies are generally reliable, but people should consider the cost of the policy and the deductible (the amount of money a policyholder must pay before the insurance payments begin). According to the Department of Justice, the average financial loss in an identity theft—including both the amount stolen and the costs associated with dealing with the theft—is $1,343. The amount many people pay for identity theft insurance might, after a couple of years, eclipse any expenses they could potentially incur through identity theft.

In addition, some banks, credit card companies, and home insurance policies already offer identity theft protection free of charge. Included in this protection are toll-free numbers to call in case of identity theft. Support is also available to help customers close accounts and file fraud reports in the case of stolen identities. While these free protection services may not dole out any financial help, they can offset the need for a lawyer.

Fraud Alerts

Under FACTA, anyone can place a fraud alert on his or her credit report, but it lasts just ninety days (unless one can prove himself or herself a victim of identity theft; then the alert lasts for seven years). A number of companies will, for a fee, extend the fraud alert past ninety days.

Fraud alerts require companies to contact an individual before issuing any new lines of credit. This prevents someone from opening new accounts without the rightful owner's knowledge. All credit approvals must come through the account holder.

Victim Assistance

Identity-theft victims can take care of resolving the crime on their own, but it takes time, effort, and money. Many reliable resources and centers (including the government's FTC) will assist victims for no charge. Other companies offer this service, but their skills and knowledge vary widely. Victims are urged to fully research these companies and investigate their claims.

Questions to Consider Before Paying for a Service

- *Does the company have a good reputation?*

- *Can you speak to other customers?*

- *Is there a refund policy?*

- *What exactly does the service provide (and not provide)?*

- *Does the company offer a trial period?*

- *Are there any long-term contracts, or can a consumer cancel at any time?*

- *What types of complaints, if any, has the company received?*

When businesses collect and store credit card and other sensitive information from customers, they can put that data at risk.

Businesses

Businesses, financial institutions, and organizations are becoming more committed to preventing identity theft in the wake of rising concerns. A recent study showed that 95 percent of people are concerned that a business will sell their personal information without permission. It's no surprise, then, that the Harvard Business Review learned in 2015 that 72 percent of Americans were hesitant to share their personal data with businesses for privacy reasons. Consumers want to know that their information will be protected.

Businesses are reacting to these consumer fears by working to build trust, and plenty of payment and money-handling services have in turn started offering different kinds of protection to businesses. In 2015, Heartland Payment Systems became the first company in the United States to offer merchants a warranty protecting them from losses in the event that their data is breached. PayPal offers seller protection and fraud prevention services. Global payment service TSYS offers a data-breach security program.

Banks can sign up for services that extend identity-theft protection to customers. This protection can include giving people access to fraud specialists; assistance with filing claims and placing fraud alerts on accounts and credit reports; and access to educational material including daily threat alerts and monthly newsletters. These services do not generally charge consumers; the banks pay for the services.

Relying Less on Social Security Numbers

Fewer businesses and agencies are using Social Security numbers to verify identities. Instead, they may assign a different set of numbers to identify individuals. Colleges, which for years used Social Security numbers on posted test score reports and identification cards, are now assigning each student a unique PIN or ID number that is not a Social Security number.

Social Security numbers are used in just one of two official ways. For one, employers use them to report data to the Social Security Administration. The agency needs to record the number of hours and years individuals work in order to calculate Social Security benefits upon retirement. In addition, Social Security numbers are used for tax-reporting purposes. Only employers, banking institutions, and select government agencies actually have a legitimate need for Social Security numbers.

Credit Card Companies

Credit cards are becoming more secure against identity fraud. In addition to the sixteen-digit number on the front of a credit card, there is another, shorter number on the back. Both numbers are usually required before a transaction can be processed. If a thief has only the sixteen-digit number, he or she can do little with it. Of course, crimes can be easily committed if a thief has both numbers or is holding the actual card.

Credit-card companies realize the risk of identity theft and the concern it poses for consumers. That is why several companies offer some type of identity theft protection, either free or for a small fee, on accounts. Most credit-card companies will assist people in filing reports, identify other attacked accounts, and monitor the case until it is closed. Some credit-card companies routinely monitor accounts for suspicious activity and notify cardholders if fraud is suspected. For additional fees, cardholders can get a higher level of protection that might include a daily monitoring of credit reports, notification if fraud is suspected, and identity theft insurance.

Government Laws and Regulations

Some laws relating to identity theft have been in place for years, while others are more recent. The high number of identity theft reports in recent years has resulted in federal and state governments taking action against the crimes. But the laws raise a host of interesting questions. How far should the government go in protecting people against identity theft? Does the law go far enough to keep information from falling into the wrong hands? Are the laws even effective? Can the average person understand the complex language in which they are written?

The Fair Credit Reporting Act

The Fair Credit Reporting Act (FCRA) was passed in 1970 in response to the fact that credit-reporting agencies were slow to act on consumer complaints. Under this law, credit-reporting agencies must investigate information that is disputed by a consumer. Information that has been deleted from an account cannot be reinserted without the consumer's knowledge. Negative information about a consumer, such as bankruptcy and tax liens, are not allowed to remain on a report indefinitely. They are generally removed within seven to ten years.

In addition, this law requires actions on the part of companies and governmental agencies that report information to credit reporting agencies. First, the information must be accurate and complete. Second, if consumers dispute information, the companies must investigate the dispute. Third, companies must notify consumers of negative information within thirty days.

The FCRA also requires that credit-reporting agencies give individuals copies of their own credit reports. However, the law's scope is surprisingly broad as to who else can obtain credit history information. For example, prospective employers can request credit reports for job applicants. The idea behind this is that employers might want to know whether a potential employee is responsible with money or can make good decisions about finances. A poor credit report may indicate otherwise. However, identity theft can affect a credit report through no fault of the individual. Employer access to a poor credit report could cost an applicant the chance for employment. Some states, concerned that this may be an invasion of privacy, are considering legislation that would limit an employer's access to credit reports. Hawaii is one state that has passed this type of legislation.

While bankruptcies more than ten years old and arrests more than seven years old generally do not appear on credit reports, the files still exist. FCRA is broad enough that some employers can request older information if the job in question pays more than $20,000 a year.

The Electronic Fund Transfer Act

This act, passed in 1978, offers consumers some protection in the case of stolen debit card information. If a victim notifies his or her financial institution of a theft within two business days, he or she is responsible for only $50, no matter how much money was fraudulently withdrawn from the account. However, a victim who waits more than two business days to report a theft may be responsible for up to $500. After sixty days, the victim could be held responsible for all the money that was stolen. It is therefore very important to keep a close tab on accounts that are tied to a debit card.

The Identity Theft and Assumption Deterrence Act

Congress passed the Identity Theft and Assumption Deterrence Act in 1998. This act contains two important provisions. First, it strengthened laws regarding identity theft criminal cases by allowing the Secret Service, the FBI, and other agencies to prosecute identity theft crimes. In addition, it required the FTC to log consumer complaints, provide victims with informational materials, and refer complaints to the proper agencies (such as consumer-reporting agencies and law enforcement officials). Based on this law, the FTC created a toll-free hotline for consumers who suspected identity theft, established a complaint database, and committed itself to educating consumers through booklets and media interviews.

This law was the first to establish that people whose identities are stolen are indeed crime victims. It was also the first law to make identity theft a crime. Under this law, if someone is convicted of using identity theft to aid in any unlawful activity, the sentence is up to fifteen years in prison and a fine.

Graham-Leach-Bliley Act

The Graham-Leach-Bliley Act of 1999 (also known as the Financial Services Modernization Act) was the first to require financial institutions to keep consumer information private. Each institution must develop privacy policies and inform consumers of those policies at least once a year. Those policies may include a more careful background check of employees with regular access to financial records, or the safeguarding of sensitive documents under lock and key.

Before this law was put in place, financial institutions routinely shared consumers' private information, not only with affiliated businesses, but also with people such as telemarketers. However, the law does not prevent financial institutions from sharing information with affiliated companies. For example, if a bank is affiliated with an insurance company, that insurance company can obtain information from the bank. However, before giving out personal financial information, the financial institution generally must let the consumer know and give the consumer the choice to "opt out" of such disclosures.

One complaint about the Graham-Leach-Bliley Act is that, while financial institutions must mail disclosures and opt-out information, customers often cannot decipher the complex language in which such notices are usually written. In fact, according to a 2014 survey conducted by the Pew Research Center, 52 percent of internet users incorrectly believed that, when they signed a privacy policy with a company, that policy ensured that their personal information would be confidential. A privacy policy, however, is simply a disclosure of how the company plans to use a customer's data. Even though there is a great deal of controversy about whether financial institutions are being misleading, proponents of the Graham-Leach-Bliley Act say that the law at least forces financial institutions to examine their privacy policies, which can result in better changes for consumers.

The USA PATRIOT Act

The USA PATRIOT Act was passed in 2001 in response to the September 11 terrorist attacks of that year. The PATRIOT Act gives the government latitude when investigating suspected or known terrorists or terrorist groups. The government implemented these rules because potential terrorists can use alternative identities to forge travel documents, and open bank accounts to access large sums of money without suspicion. In 2003, PATRIOT Act rules were finalized to require financial institutions to do three things: one, verify the identity of people opening new accounts; two, keep records of account holders so identities can be verified regularly and quickly; and three, cross-reference account holders with government-provided lists of known or suspected terrorists or terrorist groups.

As with many provisions of the PATRIOT Act, those items addressing identity theft cause controversy. Broadly, civil libertarians worry that the PATRIOT Act gives government agencies too much latitude when it comes to investigating people they consider "suspicious." How does one define "suspicious behavior"? Can someone with a personal vendetta against another person flag him or her for being "suspicious" and initiate an unjustified invasion of privacy?

FBI agents can request financial records through a court order for any investigation into suspected terrorist or intelligence-gathering activities. Under this law, when federal agents request documents from financial institutions, those working at the financial institutions are under a "gag order" to not tell anyone that the documents were requested—not even the account holder. The secret nature of these searches generally arouses the most controversy.

Sometimes, however, agents do not even need a court order to obtain financial records. If an agent deems the records important to national security, he or she simply has to make a written request. These letters are called National Security Letters (NSLs). Anyone who releases these documents to federal agents is under a gag order as well.

FACTA (or the FACT Act)

For many years, it was difficult for victims and law enforcement officials to obtain documents (such as account statements showing fraudulent charges) that showed proof of identity-theft crimes. Often, police officers had to go through the cumbersome process of obtaining search warrants through court orders to obtain the information. FACTA, passed by large majorities in the House and Senate in December 2003 and put into effect a year later, helps identity theft victims on many levels.

FACTA was passed as an amendment to the Fair Credit Reporting Act because key provisions of the FCRA were set to expire. Legislators feared that if this were allowed to happen, states would start passing their own laws regarding consumer rights and privacy, and those laws might conflict with one another.

The act protects victims by making it easier to report identity theft and set up alerts. For example, a victim needs to make just one call to set up a national fraud alert on his or her credit reports. Based on this call, creditors must contact the victim before setting up new accounts or making changes to existing accounts. As soon as one credit bureau confirms the fraud, a notice is automatically sent to the other two major credit bureaus. The victim will then receive, for free, a credit report from each agency.

The act also makes it easier for victims to get information pertaining to the fraudulent transactions. The free credit report allows people to easily obtain their records and keep a closer watch on their accounts. If a victim files a police report, the fraudulent information can be blocked from credit reports. What's more, FACTA states that victims as well as law enforcement officials have a right to obtain financial documents within thirty days of the receipt of their request. FACTA makes it possible for victims to obtain information related to the theft of their identity without relying on police departments to get those important documents.

Under the law, debt collectors have to report fraudulent information to creditors, and creditors and lenders must take action if they receive a report of fraud, even if the victim does not recognize it yet.

FACTA has changed the way credit card numbers are printed on receipts. Prior to the law, entire sixteen-digit credit card numbers were printed on receipts for merchandise and other items. But now, only the last five digits are permitted to appear, making it more difficult for thieves to obtain account information from receipts. For their part, credit reports may not show more than the last four digits of a Social Security number.

Some have argued that consumers are limited when it comes to noticing identity theft. Businesses are often in a better position to flag identity theft before a consumer even suspects it is happening. As a result, in May 2009, guidelines called "red flag rules" were added to FACTA. These rules require banks to carefully watch for address changes on existing customer accounts, or to take notice when an address provided on a new account differs from the address provided by a credit bureau. Businesses and organizations must have a written plan stating how they will combat and flag identity-theft cases. The idea behind the rules is to report suspicious activity before it becomes a full-blown, and costly, case of identity theft. Businesses are already required to protect personal information, but these rules added another layer in trying to prevent identity theft. Financial institutions, such as banks, and creditors (anyone who offers services first and sends a bill later) are expected to follow the red flag rules.

These types of businesses are required to follow four steps in order to comply with the 2009 rules:

1. *Identify the types of identity-theft red flags the business is likely to come across.*

2. *Set up procedures that will help find suspicious activity on a day-to-day basis.*

3. *Take appropriate action if red flags are discovered.*

4. *Keep a written record of the program and update it frequently.*

Breach Laws

Data breaches occur when large numbers of personal records are exposed publicly or fall into the wrong hands. Just because information has been breached does not automatically mean that it will be used to perpetrate identity theft, but it certainly opens the door and makes identity theft more likely to happen.

Many states have passed breach laws that address this growing problem. Breach laws require companies, financial institutions, organizations, and governmental agencies to report data breaches to affected consumers. In July 2003, California was the first state to pass a breach law. Nearly all states—forty-eight out of fifty, in addition to the District of Columbia, Puerto Rico, Guam, and the Virgin Islands—had enacted breach laws. In March of 2018, data breach notification laws were pending in the last two states, Alabama and South Dakota.

However, many businesses support a federal law that would standardize data breach notification rules, and no such law has yet been enacted. The first breach notification bill was introduced in Congress in 2003, and since then, many such bills have been introduced and have failed to pass. In the face of ever-larger breaches, the Data Security and Breach Notification Act was introduced in Congress on November 30, 2017; under the bill, executives who don't report breaches in a timely fashion would face up to five years in prison. The future of this bill, however, remains uncertain.

In the event of a breach, consumers are often told that it is a good idea to close the account and open up a new account with new account numbers. In some cases, it is simply recommended that they change their passwords and usernames immediately.

Freeze Laws

A freeze law enables victims to put a freeze on their credit reports. This means that no new lines of credit can be opened because an individual's credit report is "frozen," or unavailable for viewing. Very few creditors will issue new accounts without first being able to check a credit report. A freeze offers people a sense of security if there is ever a time when personal information seems particularly vulnerable (that is, when a person knows that someone is using his or her information, or if personal information has been breached). However, a freeze also means that the individual cannot obtain new credit. If an individual knows that he or she will be applying for credit, a mortgage, a car loan, or the like, a freeze may not be the best option at the time. It is possible to "thaw" a frozen report for a period of time, but the process can take a few days.

All fifty states and the District of Columbia have passed freeze laws. Freeze laws vary from state to state, so it is important to check each state's law. Some states allow only identity-theft victims to place freezes on credit reports, while other states let all consumers place freezes. Some states require consumers to pay a fee for freezes and/or thaws, while in other states, the freeze is free. Controversy over such fees arose in Washington state in

2018, as lawmakers attempted to outlaw them. At least three such bills have been introduced in Congress with the goal of making them free nationwide.

Encryption Laws

Some states are starting to enact encryption laws. These laws go one step beyond the breach laws, which simply require businesses to notify customers of data breaches. Encryption laws actually require businesses that retain personal and financial information to use software or other devices that protects the information. Encryption makes the data useless and unreadable without a password or another way to access the information. Nevada and Massachusetts were among the first states to adopt such laws. In these states, any business, no matter how big or small, must encrypt personal information and credit-card data for transactions that are done electronically.

These state-specific laws affect any business that has customers in those states. For example, if a company based in Indiana has information about a Massachusetts resident, that information needs to be encrypted even though the company itself is not in Massachusetts. Identity theft protection advocates praise these new laws, while some businesses—especially small businesses—worry about the expense involved when investing in encryption software. Smaller businesses may have to spend a few thousand dollars up front to comply, while larger businesses with many employees and computers may have to invest tens of thousands of dollars.

On the other hand, several state data-breach notification laws exempt companies whose data was encrypted from notifying consumers and the public of such breaches. Encryption, then, while it keeps data safer, may also sometimes be used to justify withholding information from those whose information has been breached.

Chapter Six

ADVANCED PREVENTION STRATEGIES

Many of the high-tech identity theft prevention methods that have been proposed or that are already being used operate on the principle that, to protect our personal information, sometimes we have to be willing to give more information. In so many aspects of our lives, data about us is compiled digitally—encrypted into magnetic strips on the back of driver's licenses, in computer databases, and stored on internet servers. Some people would argue that there should be less available information about us. After all, in many cases, we are not in control of this data and how it is used. It is compiled by others—government agencies or financial institutions—about us. Should someone other than us have control of our information? What

Opposite: As methods of identity theft become more high-tech, more complex prevention methods have become necessary.

are the dangers? Others think that more information will help verify our identities and protect us from thieves. After all, they argue, a thief cannot mimic someone's fingerprint or tone of voice—at least, not yet.

Biometrics

Biometrics is a relatively new field in which physical characteristics are used to verify a person's identity. These physical characteristics are converted into data and stored in a database. Thieves sometimes use physical characteristics to access identities. Not only are Social Security numbers and account numbers vulnerable—with biometrics, our physical information is vulnerable to attack as well. Widespread use of biometrics would someday reduce the need for people to carry around credit cards or enter account information online to make purchases. It could even eliminate the use of identifying numbers in general—from Social Security numbers and PINs to military identification numbers. We're already seeing widespread use of biometrics today in the fingerprint-login, voice recognition, and facial recognition software on our phones and other devices.

Some people contend that biometric technology is a safe, nearly foolproof way to verify someone's identity. A 2017 survey found that 86 percent of American consumers expressed interest in biometrics as a means of verifying identity or making payments. Seven in ten said that biometrics are easier to use than passwords, and 46 percent believed them to be more secure than PINs or passwords.

On the other hand, privacy advocates worry that this information can fall into the wrong hands. Will identification through physical characteristics result in bias according to race or gender? What is to stop law enforcement agencies from secretly using (or misusing) the information in crime investigations?

Members of the public are rightly concerned about how much private information should be gathered and how it will be treated.

It is important first to understand the different aspects of biometrics and how physical information can be used in different ways to verify identity.

Fingerprinting

When was the last time you used your own fingerprint to log on to your phone, download an app, or make a purchase online? While this identification method is only a few years old in the sphere of smartphones, fingerprinting has in fact been in use for many decades, most often to identify and catch criminals. Today, officials are looking toward fingerprinting as a way to safeguard identities. For example, a motor vehicles department could retain a database of fingerprints and ask people to scan their fingerprints when applying for a driver's license.

Companies and government agencies are using fingerprint technology to verify employee identities and to perform background checks. For example, before hiring teachers and other staff members, school districts often require background checks to be done by the use of fingerprinting. Prospective employees have to agree to the checks. If they refuse, they can be denied the job. Because so much identity theft occurs in the workplace, a more secure background check that uses fingerprints can screen out job candidates with questionable backgrounds. Using fingerprint identity checks in the workplace can also make facilities more secure and lessen the threat that unauthorized users will gain access to computers or areas where sensitive information is stored.

Fingerprints also enable customers to pay by touch instead of carrying cash or credit cards. In this method, the fingerprint is linked to account information, so that the bill's total is automatically withdrawn from the account. Although it

Biometric Exit

In 2003, Congress charged the US Department of Homeland Security (DHS) with designing a system for identifying travelers based on their biometric information. In 2013, US Customs and Border Protection took control of the project, called Biometric Exit. It uses facial-matching technology to identify visa holders. If passengers' faces don't match visa photos, that will be used as evidence that they may have entered the country without the proper documentation.

In 2017, US Customs and Border Protection confirmed that a database of visa holders' photos was complete. Systems had already been tested at Dulles Airport in Washington, DC, and John F. Kennedy Airport in New York City. However, in June 2017, there were reports that DHS had started scanning American citizens' faces as well.

"Treating U.S. citizens like foreign nationals contradicts years of congressional mandates," wrote Harrison Rudolph in *Slate*. "DHS has never consulted the American public about whether Americans should be subject to face recognition. That's because Congress has never given Homeland Security permission to do it in the first place." Rudolph added that, with error rates as high as 4 percent, people could miss their flights—or worse—because of misidentification. The question of who must give permission for the collection and use of such personal information remains at the heart of the biometrics debate.

is common to make purchases on a mobile device in this way, this payment option has been slow to catch on in brick-and-mortar stores because of privacy concerns and expense. For a while, some stores across the nation—select Cub Foods stores and Jewel-Osco stores—were using pay-by-touch technology. However, the company offering the technology went out of business in 2008. Financial institutions, though, have found similar technology useful. In 2017, about fifty credit unions and banks around the world were using palm authentication technology, which reads and identifies the vein patterns in individuals' palms.

The main argument against using fingerprints or similar biometrics to verify identity is the concern that fingerprints will be used in other ways. Privacy advocates want to know that fingerprint information will not be shared in violation of individuals' constitutional right to privacy. For example, what if the Federal Bureau of Investigation seeks fingerprint records to pursue criminal probes, or the Immigration and Naturalization Service wants the data to verify citizenship status?

Retinal Scans and Iris Recognition

It may sound like something from a futuristic movie, but technology can be used to scan eyes to provide another layer of identity theft protection. Parts of the eyes scanned include the retina and the iris.

A retinal scan uses technology to look at a person's eyeball, quickly measuring patterns of blood vessels that are unique to each individual. Retinal scans are generally reliable, as eyes do not change (though problems such as glaucoma and cataracts can interfere with readings). A retinal scan, however, is expensive and time-consuming. A person being scanned must sit still for several moments while an infrared beam scans the eye. In the future, computers may be outfitted with retinal-scan capabilities to verify identities for people shopping or banking online.

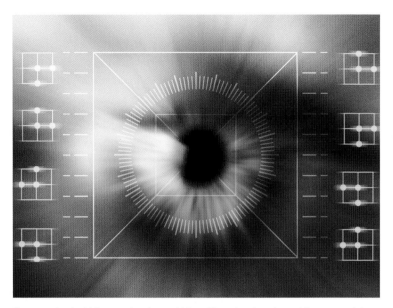

One method of biometrics-based identification involves iris-recognition or retinal-scan technology, which treats a person's eye much like a fingerprint, unique only to them.

Iris-recognition technology is a bit simpler than retinal-scan technology. In an iris scan, a video camera takes a picture of a person's iris. An iris—the colored part of the eye—is unique to each individual. However, if a pupil is dilated or if a person is wearing colored contact lenses, the information is less reliable.

Many companies have begun to offer iris-recognition software to financial institutions as a way to fight identity theft. Cairo Amman Bank in Jordan was the first to enable customers to use iris scans as a way to verify identity to withdraw money from accounts instead of swiping a card.

Voice Verification

Voice recognition allows people to identify themselves through their voice. However, this technology has a few drawbacks. Voices change over time, much more than a fingerprint or an eye scan does. Voices can be imitated. This may be especially easy with the continued development of VoCo, a new technology introduced at the Adobe MAX 2016 conference that, using only a relatively small sample of recordings of a person's voice, can change what the person says. The pitch for the product, which put a great number of people on edge, was "VoCo can make anyone say anything."

"Imagine the social engineering implications of an attacker on the telephone being able to impersonate someone the victim knows," wrote IBM Resilient CTO Bruce Schneier in response. "I don't think we're ready for this."

DNA Testing

Another controversial method of identity verification is the use of DNA testing. DNA is obtained physically through a blood sample, a cheek swab, or a strand of hair. DNA testing can be used to obtain genetic information, such as verifying the identity of a person's parents.

Several years ago, it was discovered that Major League Baseball officials were using DNA testing to verify the identities and ages of foreign baseball prospects. In the past, players from outside the United States have used forged birth certificates to claim they are younger than they really are. A sixteen-year-old player looks more promising to officials—and may be offered a more lucrative, longer contract—than a nineteen-year-old or twenty-year-old player. To get around these forgeries, baseball prospects from foreign countries are subjected to DNA tests that confirm their age. In some cases, these players are also subjected to bone scans.

Opponents of such tests worry that they will be used to predict future medical conditions. For example, DNA information can reveal a susceptibility to cancer or injury—information that team officials might take into consideration when offering someone a contract.

When it comes to using DNA testing on a broader scale for the purposes of proving people's identities, such information could also be used in unethical ways—to make hiring decisions, for example, based on a person's health or likelihood of suffering from a particular disease. The 2008 Genetic Information Nondiscrimination Act (GINA) outlawed the use of genetic information, usually acquired through DNA testing, by employers and health insurance companies. However, GINA does not apply to certain types of insurance, such as life insurance, to schools, or to housing and mortgage lenders.

Skeptics also worry that, if such information were manipulated, it would be even more difficult to prove one's identity. Scientists have shown that it is possible—even easy—to manipulate blood samples and falsify a crime scene. When it comes to fingerprints, we leave copies everywhere, on everything from door handles to the glass we drank from at lunch, making it possible for people to access them. "You may be able to get a new credit card in two weeks once you have all the information to the bank or credit issuing authority," reasons Jake Stroup in the *Balance*, "but who will issue you a new set of fingerprints to replace the stolen ones?"

A National Identification Card

Every so often, debate arises in the United States about the need for a national identity card. A national identity card would use fingerprints or other biometric information to verify the identity of the cardholder. While the idea has taken off in Europe, debate has stalled in the United States because of privacy concerns.

Driver's licenses are often used to verify identity, but not everyone has a driver's license. Social Security numbers, too, are used to identify people, but fewer governmental agencies and businesses are relying on these numbers. Such documents are also easily forged. Terrorists who want to gain access to secure areas can obtain multiple forged driver's licenses by faking birth certificates. Many argue that, by tying biometric information to an identity card, the risk of forgery goes down.

In the days after the September 11 terrorist attacks in the United States, leading politicians and bureaucrats said that if everyone presented a national identity card before boarding a plane, risks of future attacks would be lessened. Advocates said the trade-off for less privacy was increased security. Some continue to believe that, while others insist that the privacy of all citizens should be top priority.

The American Civil Liberties Union (ACLU) points out five problems that a national ID system would present. First, the ACLU argues, they can still be falsified and therefore would not solve the problem they're meant to solve. Second, they would lead the United States down "a slippery slope of surveillance and monitoring of citizens." Third, the creation of a database containing information of all Americans with cards would create new privacy problems (and security risks, for those concerned about identity theft). Fourth, they could be used to monitor the movement of citizens, another privacy concern. Finally, they would exacerbate race- and gender-based discrimination and harassment. Finding the right balance between privacy and security remains an ongoing quest.

Chapter Seven

IDENTITY THEFT ON A GLOBAL SCALE

*B*loomberg *Businessweek* reported that the 2017 attack on Equifax that compromised the records of 145.5 million people had "the hallmarks of state-sponsored pros." After the initial breach, the attack was handed off to another team of hackers, and while many of the tools utilized during the attack were Chinese, one person involved in the investigation told the magazine that this doesn't necessarily implicate China. This is not the only hack considered to be part of a larger web of state-sponsored infiltration on private data. The US government alleges that Russia was responsible for a Yahoo hack in 2014. That same year, the US Department of Justice indicted five Chinese military officers for allegedly stealing data from several US unions and companies. In December 2016, one billion Yahoo

Opposite: In 2014, a City of London police officer leads away a man suspected of participating in an international cybercrime ring charged with stealing the identity information of StubHub users.

accounts were hacked; five hundred million had been hacked just four months before, an attack that the company believed was potentially orchestrated by "the same state-sponsored hacker." China, Russia, and other accused governments have generally denied involvement in such hacking, even threatening to retaliate should such charges be pursued in a court of law. However, one thing is certain: identity theft on a massive scale has become a tool for political maneuvering on a global scale. In 2016, however, China and the United States signed an agreement not to spy on one another, and according to cybersecurity software company Symantec, there are signs that some criminal activity has declined.

Just as hackers can be from anywhere, victims can too. Around the world, consumers lose up to $575 billion per year to cybercrime. As the internet collapses geographic boundaries, identity thieves are more capable than ever of working from anywhere. They can just as easily obtain information about someone halfway around the globe as about a neighbor down the street.

Countries in Comparison

The United States led the world in number of stolen identities and number of data breaches in 2016. Symantec attributed this to three factors: high technological adoption rates, high population, and large quantity of businesses. France and Russia filled out the top three, which all owed their high number of identity thefts to megabreaches. In fact, nine in ten stolen identities in the United States in 2016 occurred in just eight large breaches. Rounding out the top ten were, in order, Canada, Taiwan, China, South Korea, Japan, the Netherlands, and Sweden. Still, the United States suffered 130 times as many compromised identities as Sweden, and nine times as many as France, which was in second place. In fact, the United States had more than twice as many identities stolen than all the other top ten countries combined.

So why does identity theft occur less in other countries than in the United States? Officials in the United States could take some ideas from European countries that might reduce instances of identity theft. The sheer number of businesses in the United States, governmental bureaucracy, and privacy concerns sometimes limit implementation of identity theft–prevention measures.

There are a few reasons Europeans are at times less vulnerable to identity theft than US residents. First, most Europeans are identified by a national identity number. This number is used far less than Social Security numbers in the United States. Europeans know to keep their identification numbers private and use them only when necessary or required by law.

Europeans also rely less on credit cards than US citizens. The average French person charges just about $267 annually to his or her credit card, compared to the average American's $4,236 in charges. If an identity thief obtains a debit card, the damage he or she can incur is usually less than is possible with a stolen credit card number. The United States has also lagged behind Europe in the implementation of security measures such as EMV and RFID microchips. It's also more likely that you'll be asked for both a microchip and a PIN (rather than a microchip and a signature) when you're making a purchase in Europe.

While highly developed countries rounded out most of the top ten countries for identity theft, other nations face their own unique challenges. In developing countries, government officials sometimes do not have the resources to investigate online fraud. This allows enterprising criminals to set up shop with little interference or oversight. Many countries have lax security or little oversight when it comes to internet security.

Laws regarding identity theft differ from country to country. Some countries, such as the United Kingdom, are already using advanced technology to combat identity theft, while others are not.

Here is a sample of how some larger, more populated countries around the world deal with identity theft.

Canada

More than 72 million Canadians' identities were stolen in 2016. Canada did not have any nationwide laws that criminalized identity theft until 2009, when three new Criminal Code offenses were passed into law. They made obtaining, possessing, or trafficking private identity information or government-issued identity documents a crime. Thieves can face up to five years in prison, and courts can also order them to pay restitution to their victim or victims. The Canadian government recommends many of the same steps to victims of identity theft as the US government does but adds that they should report the theft to the Canadian Anti-Fraud Center, which is tasked with collecting all fraud-related information.

In 2014, a new antispam law came into effect in Canada. It is now illegal to send commercial emails, text messages, and social media messages to people without their permission. In 2015, it became illegal to install programs on someone's computer with their consent, effectively making malware illegal.

Credit reports in Canada are quite similar to those in the United States, and come from such agencies as TransUnion Canada and Equifax Canada.

United Kingdom

In 2016, the United Kingdom had the second-most data breaches of any country in the world with thirty-eight—still just a fraction of the 1,023 breaches in the United States. The UK didn't make the top-ten list for countries falling victim to identity theft, and the BBC reports that the country had 172,919 incidents of fraud in 2016.

Vladimir Anikeyev (*right*), leader of a hacking collective known as Shaltai Boltai, was sentenced to two-and-a-half years in a penal colony by a Moscow court in 2017 for illegally accessing the private data of businesspeople, journalists, and government officials.

The United Kingdom's rules regarding identity theft are a little different from those in the United States. In the case of stolen credit-card information, the victim first reports the crime to the credit-card company. The company is responsible for investigating the crime and clearing the victim's record. It may elect to report the incident to the local law-enforcement agency, but it is not required to do so. If the crime does not involve credit cards, it still is reported first to whatever relevant organization was involved in the crime, and then to the local police. The burden of investigating the theft is taken off the consumer, unlike in the United States. This leads to a question: Who is better suited to report and investigate identity theft, consumers or financial institutions?

The United Kingdom is one country that has talked about using national identity cards to verify a person's identity. Each card would be linked to a biometric record of a person's face and fingerprints. The program's intent is to reduce the risk of identity theft and eliminate the need for a person to carry around several identifying documents. Sweden and Finland are two other European countries that use smart cards as national identification.

National IDs and smart cards tend to find success in Europe because of the relative ease of instituting them. For example, just five or six banking institutions dominate the European financial market; in contrast, the United States has more than ten thousand banks. So one bank in Europe that wants to implement smart-card technology immediately reaches a large segment of the population. Smart cards actually started in Europe with nationally run telephone companies. If people wanted to make a phone call, they had to use a smart card, putting smart cards in the hands of millions of customers all at once.

However, the United Kingdom is not without large identity theft crime rings, which can also be found in the United States and in other parts of the world. For example, in 2005 it was revealed that businessman Anton Gelonkin had used the identities of hundreds of dead children to defraud Britons of millions of dollars for his crime ring.

In 2008, the United Kingdom formed the National Fraud Strategic Authority (NFSA) to combat identity theft. The NFSA is charged with making the country less hospitable to identity theft crimes. The organization looks at ways to fight identity theft and protect the public. Because of the new measures, in one year the Metropolitan Police Service stopped ten separate criminal networks in London that were creating false identity cards. These criminals were charged under the 2006 Identity Cards Acts, which prohibits the use of false identity documents.

Hong Kong

Hong Kong is one of Asia's biggest finance hubs, and as a result it has seen an increase in identity-theft reports. TransUnion Hong

Kong, the country's only credit reporting agency, holds four million records. It reported just twenty cases of identity theft in the first three months of 2009. That year, police uncovered a large gang operation that was stealing financial information to commit fraud totaling $80,000. By 2017, more than 40 percent of Hong Kong residents had been, or had known, victims of identity theft.

Hong Kong officials urge people to beware of phishing schemes and never to reveal personal financial information over the phone or the internet. In 2017, seven in ten residents said they were cautious in protecting their private data, but less than half were fully aware of such long-term impacts as a poor credit score.

Since 2003, Hong Kong residents have been able to obtain credit reports, much as US citizens can. Hong Kong officials also urge residents to check credit reports to see if anything is amiss regarding their financial records.

China

Identity theft in China is often motivated by the desire to obtain jobs and education. China's government system has led to widespread corruption and abuses of power, which can breed identity theft. A few cases serve as good examples.

In 2004, Luo Caixia, a top student, was admitted to Guizhou Normal University. However, Luo never received her admittance letter and believed that she had not been accepted. Unknown to her, a classmate named Wang Jiajun took her place and attended the university under Luo's name. Meanwhile, Luo was accepted by another university. She did not learn of the identity theft until several years later, when she tried to open a bank account and was told her personal information was already in use.

It was discovered that Wang Jiajun's father, Wang Zhengrong, had paid to have the identities of the girls switched so that his daughter—who had poor grades—could go to college. The father was a local police official and was detained on charges of using his power to forge documents. The case has sparked nationwide media attention in China. While similar cases in the past have resulted in just small fines or no punishment at all, Wang Zhengrong's detention was seen as a signal that abuses of authority will no longer be tolerated.

Identity theft in China was up sharply in 2016. Chinese police arrested 4,261 suspects in 1,886 identity-theft cases just that year, compared to just 260 prosecutions between 2010 and 2014. According to one estimate, victims suffered $13.2 billion in losses. Many alleged thieves were insiders in their respective industries, including banking and e-commerce. Increased thefts may be partly attributable to the fact that huge companies such as the online retailer Alibaba Group Holding Ltd. are allowed to disclose customer information to as many third-party vendors as they like, according to their service agreement.

Australia

The Australian government recognizes the damage that identity theft inflicts upon its citizens and is taking new measures to limit instances of identity theft within the country's borders. The Identity Security branch of the Australian Attorney General's office is responsible for implementing strategies that reduce the risk of identity theft.

The government has launched a National Identity Security Strategy, which promotes the idea of a national identity card and biometric security measures. In addition, a document-verification service is a secure online database used by governmental agencies to check the accuracy and legitimacy of documents presented as proof of identity. The government has also created an identity-theft kit available to all Australians that educates them about identity theft, how to prevent it, and what steps to take if it happens.

Bulletproof Hosting

One of the largest and most notorious internet-based identity-fraud crime rings a decade ago was known as the Russian Business Network (RBN). Although the network has purportedly been offline since 2007, its influence remains today in the form of a market it helped pioneer: bulletproof hosting.

Little is known about the RBN, which was rumored to have operated out of St. Petersburg, Russia. Its internet domains were registered to anonymous addresses, and its transactions were untraceable. The RBN sold website hosting for gangs and individuals who used the sites to commit crimes. This criminal activity can take many forms, including identity theft scams. Those operating through RBN-run websites were thought to be responsible for half of all phishing schemes, security experts at the time reported. In 2006, users of the network managed to steal $150 million from bank accounts. While, by 2017, the RBN hadn't been in operation for a decade, some argued that elements of the group are likely still active, especially in the bulletproof hosting business.

Regular web hosting basically involves a collection of servers that store website content and information; most of them have restrictions on what type of content they'll agree to host, so sites involved in illegal activity such as drug dealing or identity theft aren't generally permitted. Bulletproof hosting services, however, are usually headquartered in countries with fewer laws related to identity theft, bribery, computing and data, and other crimes. In 2018, most of them were in Russia, China, and such former Soviet states as Ukraine and Moldova.

It's not easy to fight back against these bulletproof hosting services. "Cross-jurisdictional issues are a big challenge," pointed out Dhia Mahjoub, a principal engineer at OpenDNA Research, in 2017.

Traveling Abroad

Does traveling make a person more vulnerable to identity theft? The simple fact is that identity theft can happen anywhere, at any time. It can happen while people are on vacation, either in their own country or in a foreign country. Foreign travel, though, may pose a higher risk for identity theft because travelers who are unfamiliar with a country and language may become distracted and less aware of their personal possessions.

Travelers should bring only necessary documents, leaving checks and extra credit cards at home. The Identity Theft Resource Center recommends that travelers do not carry any documents that list their Social Security numbers. At the same time, alert your credit-card companies and bank where, specifically, you'll be using cards during your trip so that purchases made in an unusual place don't prompt your bank to freeze your account, and so that the bank can detect unusual spending quickly if it doesn't correspond to where you're traveling.

Keep careful watch over laptops, wallets, and purses. In hotel rooms, take advantage of a room safe if there is one, and lock all personal possessions and documents in the safe when you are not in the room. Be aware of and alert to all surroundings. Sometimes tourists are easy to spot, making them likely victims for pickpockets. Know where personal items are at all times and keep them in a secure place on the body when out in public.

Keep photocopies of important documents, such as driver's licenses and passports, and store them in a separate location from the originals. Travel can become difficult and problematic if these identity documents are stolen.

Back at home, make sure mail and newspaper delivery are put on hold or collected by a neighbor. Mail that piles up in mailboxes is an easy target for identity thieves. A mound of newspapers outside a front door provides a signal to thieves that you're not home. They may break in and steal not only possessions but also identifying documents they find lying around.

Tracking Down International Identity Theft

Officials in the United States have the authority to pursue international criminals when identity theft is perpetrated upon US citizens. US law enforcement officials work with officers of Interpol, which is an international criminal police organization. Interpol represents 188 countries.

In 2018, the Department of Justice charged thirty-six people for participation in an international identity theft crime ring that had stolen Social Security numbers, credit card information, and other private data. "We have victims in all fifty states and throughout the world," Deputy Assistant Attorney General David Rybicki reported. "It's really a standout in terms of the amount of damage that it caused." Losses were estimated at $530 million. The indictment alleged that the organization, called Infraud, had been established by a Ukrainian national in 2010. More than ten thousand people had been involved in trading the private data. Many of those charged faced at least twenty years in prison.

Those seeking to fight back against identity theft have seen many successes like these, but there are more obstacles ahead as criminals continue to adapt and invent new strategies, and law enforcement and security professionals keep innovating new ways to stop them. Even with these protections in place, every individual has an important role to play in protecting his or her identity and the identities of others.

Glossary

ATM An acronym for "automated teller machine," a computerized electronic machine used to perform basic banking transactions.

consumer Any person that utilizes economic goods—for instance, by making purchases.

dark web An online marketplace where people buy and sell illegal goods and services.

data breach An unauthorized incursion into a database, usually collected and maintained by a business or government agency, containing the private information of a large number of people for the purpose of stealing that information.

electronic health record Electronically captured data about a medical patient that can be shared digitally between doctors and hospitals.

Federal Trade Commission A government agency, abbreviated as the FTC, whose primary goals are to protect consumers and prevent monopolies.

loophole An ambiguity or omission in a text via which the intent of a law or contract can be evaded.

malware Software designed to interfere with the way a computer normally functions in a way that is in some manner detrimental to the computer's owner or to another person.

phishing A strategy whereby an identity thief attempts to trick a target into revealing personal information, usually via email messages or phone calls.

PIN An acronym for "personal identification number," a code used in combination with a debit or credit card to access an account, often at an ATM.

precaution Care taken in advance to ensure that something bad doesn't happen.

private Intended for or restricted to the use of a particular person, group, or class.

ransomware A type of malware that requires a victim to pay a ransom in exchange for restoring their access to encrypted files.

rationalization The action of attempting to explain or justify behavior or an attitude with logical reasons, even if these are not appropriate.

skimmer A device that is used to scan and steal credit card information without ever coming in contact with the card.

social engineering A strategy of stealing people's identities by compiling seemingly innocent information, such as a pet's name or a child's birth date, to unlock more useful data, such as stolen account information.

spyware A type of malware that is installed on a computer without the owner's permission and transmits information about the computer's online activities.

subpoena An official document requiring that a person appear in court.

two-factor authentication A method of ensuring that a person attempting to access an account is, indeed, the account owner whereby a password is combined with authentication using a device, such as a smartphone, that only the rightful user should have access to.

Further Information

Books

Chappell, Robert P. Jr. *Child Identity Theft: What Every Parent Needs to Know*. Lanham, MD: Rowman & Littlefield Publishers, 2012.

LaVine, Howard. *How to Increase Online Security With Smartphones, Tablets and Computers*. Amazon Digital Services LLC, 2014.

McNally, Megan. *Identity Theft in Today's World*. Santa Barbara, CA: Praeger, 2012.

Singer, P.W., and Allan Friedman. *Cybersecurity and Cyberwar: What Everyone Needs to Know*. New York: Oxford University Press, 2014.

Websites

Experian

http://www.experian.com

As one of the three major credit-reporting agencies in the United States, Experian's site contains a great deal of educational information on fraud and identity theft. You can also run a free dark web scan to see if your information has been shared there.

Identity Theft Resource Center

http://www.idtheftcenter.org

The Identity Theft Resource Center, based in San Diego, California, shares a variety of information including the latest scam alerts, state and local resources, and statistics. The organization provides a toll-free number that victims can call if they've been targeted by identity thieves. The number is (888) 400-5530.

Privacy Rights Clearinghouse

http://www.privacyrights.org

The Privacy Rights Clearinghouse was founded in 1992 and is dedicated to giving consumers information about their privacy rights.

Videos

Catch Me If You Can

http://www.imdb.com/title/tt0264464

This 2002 film starring Leonardo DiCaprio is based on the true story of Frank Abagnale Jr., who stole millions of dollars via identity theft.

Five Ways to Help Protect Your Identity

https://www.youtube.com/watch?v=lp_8cvNm_vE

This video from the Federal Trade Commission outlines ways to make keeping your identity secure a part of your daily routine.

How to File a Complaint with the Federal Trade Commission

https://www.youtube.com/watch?v=3LvMO5UMCl8&feature=youtu.be

This Federal Trade Commission video explains how to file a complaint of identity theft.

Organizations

Canadian Anti-Fraud Centre

PO Box 686

North Bay, ON P1B 8J8

(888) 495-8501

http://www.antifraudcentre-centreantifraude.ca

The Canadian Anti-Fraud Centre is the primary Canadian agency tasked with compiling information and on such matters as mass marketing fraud, internet fraud, and complaints of identity theft.

Federal Trade Commission

600 Pennsylvania Avenue, NW

Washington, DC 20580

(202) 326-2222

http://www.ftc.gov/idtheft

As the agency responsible for protecting US consumers when it comes to financial and monetary issues, the FTC offers a wealth of information on its website.

National Association of Attorneys General

1850 M Street NW, 12th floor

Washington, DC 20036

(202) 326-6000

http://www.naag.org

In each state, an attorney general oversees state laws as they relate to consumers. An attorney general's website will often give consumers information about the latest scams (identity scams and others) and provide a number or web address for lodging complaints.

National Crime Prevention Council

2614 Chapel Lake Drive, Suite B

Gambrills, MD 21054

(443) 292-4565

http://www.ncpc.org

This organization provides a wealth of information on everything from cybercrimes to intellectual property theft.

Royal Canadian Mounted Police

Headquarters Building

73 Leikin Drive

Ottawa, ON K1A 0R2

http://www.rcmp-grc.gc.ca/scams-fraudes/id-theft-vol-eng.htm

This organization provides key information for Canadians who have become the victims of identity fraud.

United States Department of Justice

950 Pennsylvania Avenue, NW
Washington, DC 20530-0001

(202) 514-2000

https://www.justice.gov/criminal-fraud/identity-theft/identity-theft-and-identity-fraud

Responsible for fighting identity theft that occurs on a federal level, the Department of Justice offers useful information on what to do if you've been the victim of identity theft.

Bibliography

Abagnale, Frank W. *Catch Me If You Can: The True Story of a Real Fake*. New York: Broadway, 2000.

"About Frank Abagnale." Abagnale and Associates. www.abagnale.com/aboutfrank.htm.

Aho, Brionna. "US Census Scams: When Fraudsters Dig Deeper." Washington State Office of the Attorney General, February 27, 2017. http://www.atg.wa.gov/all-consuming-blog/us-census-scams-when-fraudsters-dig-deeper.

Aimoto, Shaun, et al. "Internet Security Threat Report: Government." Symantec Corporation, June 2017. https://www.symantec.com/content/dam/symantec/docs/reports/gistr22-government-report.pdf.

Ambrose, Eileen. "College Students Should Study up on ID Theft." *Chicago Tribune*, September 7, 2008. http://articles.chicagotribune.com/2008-09-07/business/0809050818_1_credit-reports-credit-bureaus-credit-card.

"Americans Taking Abramoff, Alito and Domestic Spying in Stride." Pew Research Center, January 11, 2006. http://people-press.org/report/267/americans-taking-abramoff-alito-and-domestic-spying-in-stride.

Arata, Michael J. Jr. *Preventing Identity Theft for Dummies*. Indianapolis, IN: Wiley Publishing, Inc., 2004.

Armerding, Taylor. "The 17 Biggest Data Breaches of the 21st Century." *CSO*, January 26, 2018. https://www.csoonline.com/article/2130877/data-breach/the-biggest-data-breaches-of-the-21st-century.html

———. "Vocal Theft on the Horizon." *CSO*, May 16, 2017. https://www. csoonline.com/article/3196820/security/vocal-theft-on-the-horizon. html.

"Banking on Biometrics in the Twinkle of an Eye. IrisGuard Is Transforming the Way We Conduct Our Banking Transactions." Business Wire, April 14, 2008. https://www.businesswire.com/news/ home/20080414005766/en/Banking-Biometrics-Twinkle-Eye.- IrisGuard-Transforming-Conduct.

Bazar, Emily. "Illegal Immigrants Are Issued ID Cards in Some Places." *USA TODAY*, October 4, 2007. www.usatoday.com/news/nation/2007-10- 03-Immigrant_N.htm.

"Belgium Sentences Fake-Id Gang Used by Brussels and Paris Attackers." BBC News, January 19, 2017. http://www.bbc.com/news/world- europe-38683199.

Bernardo, Richie. "2017's States Most Vulnerable to Identity Theft & Fraud." *WalletHub*, October 18, 2017. https://wallethub.com/edu/ states-where-identity-theft-and-fraud-are-worst/17549.

Blakely, Rhys, Jonathan Richards, and Tony Halpin. "Cybergang Raises Fear of New Crime Wave." *Times* (UK), November 10, 2007. https:// www.thetimes.co.uk/article/cybergang-raises-fear-of-new-crime- wave-6frpspqlx2t.

Bolden-Barrett, Valerie. "Study: 68% of HR Managers See Identity Theft Protection as a Vital Benefit." *HR Dive*, October 2, 2017. https:// www.hrdive.com/news/study-68-of-hr-managers-see-identity-theft- protection-as-a-vital-benefit/506209.

Bradley, Tony. "Stalled Equifax Breach Investigation Could Provide Valuable Insight." *Forbes*, February 20, 2018. https://www.forbes.com/sites/

tonybradley/2018/02/20/stalled-equifax-breach-investigation-could-provide-valuable-insight/#687f4516d819.

Brandom, Russell. "Facial Recognition Is Coming to US Airports, Fast-Tracked by Trump." *Verge*, April 18, 2017. https://www.theverge.com/2017/4/18/15332742/us-border-biometric-exit-facial-recognition-scanning-homeland-security.

Calos, Katherine. "Census workers mindful of identity theft fears." *Richmond Times-Dispatch,* May 5, 2009. http://www.richmond.com/news/census-workers-mindful-of-identity-theft-fears/article_44cfeec3-3a8f-5c59-b62f-d81ef6e48e45.html.

Chalfant, Morgan. "DOJ Charges 36 in Global Cyber Crime Ring Takedown." *Hill*, February 7, 2018. http://thehill.com/policy/cybersecurity/372756-officials-charge-36-in-massive-international-cybercrime-ring-takedown.

Collins, Judith M. *Investigating Identity Theft: A Guide for Businesses, Law Enforcement, and Victims*. Hoboken, NJ: John Wiley & Sons, 2006.

"Consumer Reports Survey: One in Five Online Consumers Have Been Victims of Cybercrime." *Consumer Reports*, May 4, 2009. https://www.consumerreports.org/media-room/press-releases/2009/05/consumer-reports-survey-one-in-five-online-consumers-have-been-victims-of-cybercrime.

"Consumers Ready to Switch from Passwords to Biometrics, Study Shows." Visa. Accessed March 7, 2018. https://usa.visa.com/visa-everywhere/security/how-fingerprint-authentication-works.html.

"Consumers Union's Guide to Security Freeze Protection." Financialprivacynow.org, April 6, 2009. http://consumersunion.org/research/consumers-unions-guide-to-security-freeze-protection-2.

"Cybertheft Case Skewers Celebs." CBSNews.com, March 20, 2001. www.cbsnews.com/stories/2001/03/20/archive/technology/ main280107.shtml

Dakss, Brian. "Kids' ID Theft: Growing Problem." CBS News Early Show, January 15, 2006. www.cbsnews.com/stories/2006/01/15/ earlyshow/living/ConsumerWatch/main1210020.shtml.

Davis, Kristina. "Mexican Man Admits He Assumed American's Identity in 1980 and Stole $361,000 in Government Benefits." *Los Angeles Times*, March 3, 2018. http://www.latimes.com/local/lanow/la-me-identity-mexican-20180303-story.html.

Dignan, Larry. "Phishing Remains a Data Breach Weapon of Choice, Says Verizon." ZDNet, April 26, 2016. http://www.zdnet.com/article/ phishing-remains-a-data-breach-weapon-of-choice-says-verizon.

Douglas-Gabriel, Danielle. "Identity Thieves May Have Hacked Files of up to 100,000 Financial Aid Applicants." *Washington Post*, April 6, 2017. https://www.washingtonpost.com/news/grade-point/wp/2017/04/06/ identity-thieves-may-have-hacked-files-of-up-to-100000-financial-aid-applicants/?utm_term=.adc2ec5c5d58.

Dugas, Christine. "More Banks Offer Free Help to Victims of Identity Theft." *USA TODAY*, January 19, 2007. www.usatoday.com/money/industries/ banking/2007-01-19-bank-id-theft_x.htm.

"Electronic Health Records (EHR) Incentive Programs." Centers for Medicare & Medicaid Services. Accessed March 4, 2018. https://www.cms.gov/Regulations-and-Guidance/Legislation/ EHRIncentivePrograms/index.html?redirect=/ehrincentiveprograms.

"Fact Sheet 106: Organizing Your Identity Theft Case." Identity Theft Resource Center, April 28, 2007. www.idtheftcenter.org/artman2/

publish/v_fact_sheets/Fact_Sheet_106_Organizing_Your_Identity_
Theft_Case.shtml.

"Fact Sheet 108: Overcoming the Emotional Impact." Identity Theft
Resource Center, April 28, 2007. https://www.idtheftcenter.org/
Identity-Theft/overcoming-the-emotional-impact-of-identity-theft.html

"Fact Sheet 115: When You Personally Know the Identity Thief." Identity
Theft Resource Center, May 2, 2007. www.idtheftcenter.org/artman2/
publish/v_fact_sheets/Fact_Sheet_115_When_you_personallyknow_
the_identity_thief.shtml.

"Fact Sheet 122: Identity Theft Travel Tips." Identity Theft Resource Center,
May 1, 2007. https://www.idtheftcenter.org/Fact-Sheets/fs-122.html.

"Fact Sheet 301: Enhancing Law Enforcement." Identity Theft Resource
Center, August 21, 2009. https://www.idtheftcenter.org/Fact-Sheets/
fs-301.html.

Federal Trade Commission. *Consumer Sentinel Network Data Book for
January–December 2008*. Washington, DC: Federal Trade Commission,
February 2009.

———. "Kids and Computer Security." Consumer Information, September
2011. https://www.consumer.ftc.gov/articles/0017-kids-and-computer-
security.

"Fighting Fraud with the Red Flags Rule: A How-To Guide for Business."
Federal Trade Commission, March 2009. https://www.ftc.gov/tips-
advice/business-center/guidance/fighting-identity-theft-red-flags-rule-
how-guide-business.

"5 Problems with National ID Cards." ACLU. Accessed March 7, 2018.
https://www.aclu.org/other/5-problems-national-id-cards.

German, Rachel. "What Are the Chances for a Federal Breach Notification Law?" The University of Texas at Austin Center for Identity. Accessed March 7, 2018. https://identity.utexas.edu/id-experts-blog/what-are-the-chances-for-a-federal-breach-notification-law.

Glater, Jonathan D. "Another Hurdle for the Jobless: Credit Inquiries." *New York Times*. August 6, 2009. www.nytimes.com/2009/08/07/business/07credit.html?_r=2&hp.

Gorodyansky, David. "3 Reasons Why Privacy Matters to Your Business, Your Brand and Your Future." *Entrepreneur*, May 9, 2017. https://www.entrepreneur.com/article/293785.

Gredler, Cody. "The Real Cost of Identity Theft." CSID, September 9, 2016. https://www.csid.com/2016/09/real-cost-identity-theft.

"Guide for Assisting Identity Theft Victims." Federal Trade Commission, September 2013. https://www.consumer.ftc.gov/articles/pdf-0119-guide-assisting-id-theft-victims.pdf.

Guzzardi, Joe. "Identity Theft an Overlooked Wrinkle of Illegal Immigration." *Jackson (FL) Sun*, July 3, 2017. http://www.jacksonsun.com/story/opinion/columnists/2017/07/03/identity-theft-overlooked-wrinkle-illegal-immigration/444863001.

Hart, Kim. "Phish-Hooked Thieves Find Easy Pickings on Social Sites." *Washington Post*, July 16, 2006. https://www.washingtonpost.com/archive/business/2006/07/16/phish-hooked-span-classbankheadthieves-find-easy-pickings-on-social-sitesspan/a4a05b30-8c46-45c2-9d30-3c8f117c5a5a/?utm_term=.80531168093c.

Hauser, Christine. "ICE Lawyer Charged with Stealing Immigrants' Identities." *New York Times*, February 14, 2018. https://www.nytimes.com/2018/02/14/us/ice-seattle-immigrant-identities.html.

Horovitz, Bruce. "Restaurants Tighten Credit Card Security." *USA TODAY*, March 5, 2007. http://www.ramw.org/news/restaurants-tighten-credit-card-security.

"'I Am You': Hear Hacker's Threats to Victim of Identity Theft." CBS News, September 25, 2017. https://www.cbsnews.com/news/i-am-you-hear-hackers-threats-to-identity-theft-victim.

"Identity and Benefit Fraud." US Immigration and Customs Enforcement, June 8, 2017. https://www.ice.gov/identity-benefit-fraud.

"Identity Fraud Hits All Time High With 16.7 Million U.S. Victims in 2017." Identity Guard, February 9, 2018. https://www.identityguard.com/press-releases/identity-fraud-hits-all-time-high-with-16-7-million-u-s-victims-in-2017-according-to-new-javelin-strategy-research-study.

"Identity Fraud Reached Record Levels in 2016." BBC News, March 15, 2017. http://www.bbc.com/news/uk-39268542.

"Identity Theft Protection Services." Federal Trade Commission, Consumer Information, March 2016. https://www.consumer.ftc.gov/articles/0235-identity-theft-protection-services.

Identity Theft Resource Center. "Identity Theft: The Aftermath 2017." 2017. https://www.idtheftcenter.org/images/page-docs/Aftermath_2017.pdf.

"Identity Theft Twice as Likely in Canada, the UK, and the US than in Other European Countries." *Canada NewsWire.* October 21, 2008. https://www.newswire.ca/news-releases/identity-theft-twice-as-likely-in-canada-the-uk-and-the-us-than-in-other-european-countries-536751341.html.

Insurance Information Institute. "Facts + Statistics: Identity Theft and Cybercrime." 2018. https://www.iii.org/fact-statistic/facts-statistics-identity-theft-and-cybercrime.

"Iona College Becomes the First to Create a 'Data Breach-Free Campus' and Provide Proactive Identity Theft Protection to Students, Faculty and Staff." *Business Wire,* March 2, 2009. https://www.businesswire.com/news/home/20090302005773/en/Iona-College-Create-%E2%80%9CData-Breach-Free-Campus%E2%80%9D-Provide

Jackman, Tom. "Fraud Inevitably Follows Disasters, so Authorities in Texas, Florida Prepare for Post-Storm Scams." *Washington Post,* September 8, 2017. https://www.washingtonpost.com/news/true-crime/wp/2017/09/08/fraud-inevitably-follows-disasters-so-authorities-in-texas-florida-prepare-for-post-storm-scams/?utm_term=.7cb981a61796.

Javelin Strategy & Research. "Identity Fraud Hits Record High with 15.4 Million U.S. Victims in 2016, Up 16 Percent According to New Javelin Strategy & Research Study." February 1, 2017. https://www.javelinstrategy.com/press-release/identity-fraud-hits-record-high-154-million-us-victims-2016-16-percent-according-new.

———. "$16 Billion Stolen from 12.7 Million Identity Fraud Victims in 2014, According to Javelin Strategy & Research." March 3, 2015. https://www.javelinstrategy.com/press-release/16-billion-stolen-127-million-identity-fraud-victims-2014-according-javelin-strategy.

Johnson, Andrew. "LifeLock Tries to Fend off Legal Battles." *Arizona Republic*, August 17, 2009. http://archive.azcentral.com/arizonarepublic/news/articles/2009/08/17/20090817biz-lifelock0817.html.

Keppler, Nick, Karen Freifeld, and John Walcott. "Siemens, Trimble, Moody's Breached by Chinese Hackers, U.S. Charges." Reuters, November 27, 2017. https://www.reuters.com/article/us-usa-cyber-china-indictments/siemens-trimble-moodys-breached-by-chinese-hackers-u-s-charges-idUSKBN1DR26D.

Kershner, Isabel. "New U.S.-Israeli Crime Ring Detailed." *New York Times*, August 3, 2009. www.nytimes.com/2009/08/04/world/middleeast/04israel.html.

Kieke, Reba L. "Although a Relatively New Risk Area, Medical Identity Theft Should Not Be Taken Lightly." *Journal of Health Care Compliance* 11, no. 1 (2009): 51–74.

Kirchheimer, Sid. "Census Scams: Hard to Detect, Easy for Fraudsters." AARP, January 30, 2015. https://blog.aarp.org/2015/01/30/census-scams-hard-to-detect-easy-for-fraudsters.

Konsko, Lindsay. "Do People in Other Countries Use Credit Cards as Much as Americans?" *NerdWallet*, February 19, 2014. https://www.nerdwallet.com/blog/credit-cards/people-countries-credit-cards-americans.

Krebs, Brian. "A Brief History of Phishing." *Washington Post*, November 18, 2004. www.washingtonpost.com/wp-dyn/articles/A59350-2004Nov18.html.

———. "Mapping the Russian Business Network." *Washington Post*, October 13, 2007. http://voices.washingtonpost.com/securityfix/2007/10/mapping_the_russian_business_n.html.

———. "Shadowy Russian Firm Seen as Conduit for Cybercrime." *Washington Post*, October 13, 2007. www.washingtonpost.com/wp-dyn/content/article/2007/10/12/AR2007101202461.html.

Lafferty, Latour. "Medical Identity Theft: The Future Threat of Health Care Fraud Is Now." *Journal of Health Care Compliance*, 2007:11–20.

LaPonsie, Maryalene. "Withdrawing Money with a Retina Scan: The Future of Biometrics and Banking." *U.S. News & World Report*, September 1,

2017. https://money.usnews.com/money/personal-finance/banking-and-credit/articles/2017-09-01/withdrawing-money-with-a-retina-scan-the-future-of-biometrics-and-banking.

Lewis, Jackson. "Alabama Senates Passes Data Breach Notification Act." Lexology, March 6, 2018. https://www.lexology.com/library/detail.aspx?g=9e5a0747-faa9-4400-95fc-d5ffe4891d05.

Leyden, John. "Bulletproof hosts stay online by operating out of disputed backwaters." *Register* (UK), October 5, 2017. https://www.theregister.co.uk/2017/10/05/bulletproof_hosting.

Light, Joe. "Children Targeted in Surging Numbers." *Boston Globe*, July 10, 2005. http://archive.boston.com/business/personalfinance/articles/2005/07/10/children_targeted_in_surging_numbers.

Liptak, Adam, and Julia Preston. "Supreme Court Hears Challenge to Identity theft Law in Immigration Cases." *New York Times*, February 25, 2009. www.nytimes.com/2009/02/26/us/26identity.html?_r=1&scp=1&sq=identity%20theft%20immigration%20supreme%20court&st=cse.

Long, Katherine. "Did You Get the Letter? WSU Sends Warning to 1 Million People after Hard Drive with Personal Info Is Stolen." *Seattle Times*, June 22, 2017. https://www.seattletimes.com/seattle-news/education/did-you-get-letter-wsu-sends-warning-to-1-million-people-after-hard-drive-with-personal-info-is-stolen.

Menn, Joseph, and Andrea Chang. "11 Charged in Massive Identity Theft." *Los Angeles Times*. August 6, 2008. http://articles.latimes.com/2008/aug/06/business/fi-hack6.

Meyer, Zlati. "1.3 Million Kids Have Identity Stolen Annually, 50% Under 6-Years-Old." *Detroit (MI) Free Press*, August 28, 2016. https://www.

freep.com/story/money/business/2016/08/28/child-id-theft-problem/89352016.

Minter, Adam. "Chinese Learning the Value of Privacy." *Japan Times*, March 25, 2017. https://www.japantimes.co.jp/opinion/2017/03/25/commentary/world-commentary/chinese-learning-value-privacy/#.WqSFw2bMzoy.

McCoy, Kevin. "Target to Pay $18.5M for 2013 Data Breach that Affected 41 Million Consumers." *USA TODAY*, May 23, 2017. https://www.usatoday.com/story/money/2017/05/23/target-pay-185m-2013-data-breach-affected-consumers/102063932.

Money Watch. "Bitcoins Worth $100K Stolen over Public Wireless Network." CBS News, November 22, 2017. https://www.cbsnews.com/news/bitcoins-worth-100k-stolen-over-public-wireless-network.

Morgan Stanley. "Child Identity Theft: A Guide for Parents." July 21, 2017. https://www.morganstanley.com/articles/child-identity-theft.

National Center on Elder Abuse. "Research: Statistics/Data." Accessed March 4, 2018. https://ncea.acl.gov/whatwedo/research/statistics.html#11.

O'Connell, Brian. "What Is Synthetic ID Theft and How Can You Protect Yourself?" Experian, November 30, 2017. https://www.experian.com/blogs/ask-experian/what-is-synthetic-id-theft-and-how-can-you-protect-yourself.

Office of the National Coordinator for Health Information Technology. "Hospitals Participating in the CMS EHR Incentive Programs." Health IT Quick-Stat #45, August 2017. https://dashboard.healthit.gov/quickstats/pages/FIG-Hospitals-EHR-Incentive-Programs.php.

Ortutay, Barbara. "Facebook Plans to Simplify Privacy Settings." ABC
    Local, July 1, 2009. http://abclocal.go.com/ktrk/story?section=news/
    technology&id=6894261

Pallister, David. "Three Guilty of Identity Fraud Which Netted
    Millions." *Guardian*. December 1, 2006. https://www.theguardian.com/
    uk/2006/dec/01/ukcrime.davidpallister.

Palmer, Danny. "1.4 Million Phishing Websites Are Created Every Month:
    Here's Who the Scammers Are Pretending to Be." ZDNet, September 22,
    2017. http://www.zdnet.com/article/1-4-million-phishing-websites-are-
    created-every-month-heres-who-the-scammers-are-pretending-to-be.

"Phishing Activity Trends Report: 2nd Half 2008." Anti-Phishing Working
    Group. www.antiphishing.org/reports/apwg_report_H2_2008.pdf.

"Phishing Schemes Make IRS 'Dirty Dozen' List of Tax Scams for 2018;
    Individuals, Businesses, Tax Pros Urged to Remain Vigilant." IRS, March
    5, 2018. https://www.irs.gov/newsroom/phishing-schemes-make-irs-
    dirty-dozen-list-of-tax-scams-for-2018-individuals-businesses-tax-pros-
    urged-to-remain-vigilant.

Ponemon Institute. "2017 Cost of Data Breach Study: United States."
    IBM, June 2017. https://www-01.ibm.com/common/ssi/cgi-bin/
    ssialias?htmlfid=SEL03130USEN&.

Renner, Kevin. "The New Rules of Identity Theft Protection for
    Employees." Corporate Wellness Magazine, 2014–2015. http://www.
    corporatewellnessmagazine.com/others/new-rules-identity-theft-
    protection.

Riley, Michael, Jordan Robertson, and Anita Sharpe. "The Equifax
    Hack Has the Hallmarks of State-Sponsored Pros." *Bloomberg
    Businessweek*, September 29, 2017. https://www.bloomberg.com/news/

features/2017-09-29/the-equifax-hack-has-all-the-hallmarks-of-
state-sponsored-pros.

Rucker, Patrick. "Exclusive: U.S. Consumer Protection Official Puts
Equifax Probe on Ice – Sources." Reuters, February 4, 2018. https://
www.reuters.com/article/us-usa-equifax-cfpb/exclusive-u-s-
consumer-protection-official-puts-equifax-probe-on-ice-sources-
idUSKBN1FP0IZ.

Rudolph, Harrison. "DHS Is Starting to Scan Americans' Faces Before
They Get on International Flights." *Slate*, June 21, 2017. http://www.
slate.com/blogs/future_tense/2017/06/21/dhs_s_biometric_exit_
program_is_starting_to_scan_americans_faces_before.html.

Sandberg, Erica. "Military Families Remain Easy Prey for ID Theft."
Creditcards.com, February 14, 2014. https://www.creditcards.com/
credit-card-news/identity_theft-military-families-1282.php.

Sausner, Rebecca. "B of A: Phishing Victims Won't Get Fooled
Again." *American Banker*, May 5, 2009. https://www.americanbanker.
com/news/b-of-a-phishing-victims-wont-get-fooled-again.

Schmidt, Michael S., and Alan Schwarz. "Baseball's Use of DNA Raises
Questions." *New York Times*, July 21, 2009. www.nytimes.
com/2009/07/22/sports/baseball/22dna.html?ref=baseball.

Schwarz, Alan. "A Future in Baseball, Hinging on DNA." *New York
Times*, July 22, 2009. www.nytimes.com/2009/07/23/sports/
baseball/23dna.html?_r=1&partner=rss&emc=rss.

"Senators Collins, McCaskill's Bill to Protect Seniors from Financial
Exploitation and Fraud Advances." Susan Collins, United States
Senator for Maine, January 29, 2018. https://www.collins.senate.gov/

newsroom/senators-collins-mccaskill's-bill-protect-seniors-financial-exploitation-and-fraud-advances.

"Shipping Board Embezzler, Killing Himself, Wrote That He Assumed a Dead Man's Name." *New York Times*, November 25, 1923. https://www.nytimes.com/1923/11/25/archives/shipping-board-embezzler-killing-himself-wrote-that-he-assumed-a.html.

"Shoppers, You Can't Touch This." *Chicago Tribune*, March 21, 2008. http://articles.chicagotribune.com/2008-03-21/news/0803210233_1_authentication-and-payment-system-jewel-biometric.

Siciliano, Robert, et al. "Identity Theft: The Aftermath 2016." Identity Theft Resource Center, 2016. https://www.ftc.gov/system/files/documents/public_comments/2017/10/00004-141445.pdf.

Silverman, Lauren. "There Are Plenty Of RFID-Blocking Products, But Do You Need Them?" NPR, July 4, 2017. https://www.npr.org/sections/alltechconsidered/2017/07/04/535518514/there-are-plenty-of-rfid-blocking-products-but-do-you-need-them.

Silverstein, Stuart. "Ex-Waitress Allegedly Swiped Patrons' Identities." *Los Angeles Times*, May 22, 2007. http://articles.latimes.com/2007/may/22/local/me-waitress22.

Smith, Aaron. "Half of Online Americans Don't Know What a Privacy Policy Is." Pew Research Center, December 4, 2014. http://www.pewresearch.org/fact-tank/2014/12/04/half-of-americans-dont-know-what-a-privacy-policy-is.

"Social Engineering, Cybercrime Will Be Challenges in 2009, Predicts Identity Theft Assistance Center." Smart Card News Online,

December 2, 2008. http://www.smartcard.co.uk/NOLARCH/2008/
December/021208.html#_2.

Social Security Legislative Bulletin. "President Signs H.R. 624, The Social
Security Number Fraud Prevention Act of 2017." Social Security,
September 19, 2017. https://www.ssa.gov/legislation/legis_
bulletin_091917.html.

Solove, Daniel J., Marc Rotenberg, and Paul M. Schwartz. *Privacy,
Information, and Technology*. New York: Aspen Publishers, 2006.

Stewart, Emily. "Elizabeth Warren Warns Equifax Could 'Wiggle off the
Hook' for Users' Credit Data Getting Hacked." *Vox*, February 7, 2018.
https://www.vox.com/policy-and-politics/2018/2/7/16984522/
elizabeth-warren-equifax-data-breach-cfpb.

———. "Equifax Compromised Half of the Country's Information. Trump's
CFPB Isn't Looking into It." *Vox*, February 5, 2018. https://www.vox.
com/policy-and-politics/2018/2/5/16974090/mick-mulvaney-cfpb-
equifax-data-breach-probe.

Stewart, Gail. *Crime Scene Investigations: Identity Theft*. San Diego, CA:
Lucent Books, 2007.

Stout, David. "Supreme Court Rules Against Government in Identity
Theft Case." *New York Times*, May 4, 2009. www.nytimes.
com/2009/05/05/us/05scotus.html.

Stroup, Jake. "Biometric Identification and Identity Theft." *Balance*,
October 5, 2017. https://www.thebalance.com/biometric-
identification-and-identity-theft-1947595.

Sullivan, Bob. "ID Thief to the Stars Tells All." MSNBC.com. www.msnbc.
msn.com/id/5763781.

————. "Identity Theft Hit an All-Time High in 2016." *USA TODAY*, February 6, 2017. https://www.usatoday.com/story/money/personalfinance/2017/02/06/identity-theft-hit-all-time-high-2016/97398548.

Sydell, Laura. "Ohio Man Charged with Putting Spyware on Thousands of Computers." NPR, All Tech Considered, January 12, 2018. https://www.npr.org/sections/alltechconsidered/2018/01/12/577761143/ohio-man-charged-with-putting-spyware-on-thousands-of-computers.

Symanovich, Steve. "W-2 Phishing Scam: What It Is and How to Help Protect Against It." LifeLock, January 25, 2018. https://www.lifelock.com/education/w-2-phishing-scam-what-it-is-and-how-to-help-protect-against-it.

Synovate. "Federal Trade Commission 2006 Identity Theft Survey Report." McLean, VA: Synovate, November 2007.

Tatham, Matt. "20 Types of Identity Theft and Fraud." Experian, January 5, 2018. https://www.experian.com/blogs/ask-experian/20-types-of-identity-theft-and-fraud.

Thimou, Theo. "Warning: Donating Your Stuff Could Leave You Open to Identity Theft." *Clark*, December 27, 2016. https://clark.com/consumer-issues-id-theft/charitable-donations-leave-you-open-identity-theft.

"Tough Identity Theft Law Passed." *CBC News*, October 27, 2009. http://www.cbc.ca/news/canada/tough-identity-theft-law-passed-1.807894.

Townsend, Mark. "Four Million Britons Have Fallen Victim to Identity Fraud. Are You Next?" *Observer*, December 9, 2007. https://www.theguardian.com/theobserver/2007/dec/09/features.magazine87.

"Treasury and Federal Financial Regulators Issue Final Patriot Act Regulations on Customer Identification." US Treasury Department, April 30, 2003. https://www.treasury.gov/press-center/press-releases/Pages/js335.aspx

Trounson, Rebecca. "FBI Site to Aid UCLA Hacker Probe." *Los Angeles Times*, December 16, 2006. http://articles.latimes.com/2006/dec/16/local/me-ucla16.

"Unisys Research Shows U.S. Consumers Overwhelmingly Trust Biometrics for Data Protection." Business Wire, December 9, 2008. https://www.businesswire.com/news/home/20081209005180/en/Unisys-Research-Shows-U.S.-Consumers-Overwhelmingly-Trust.

Vacca, John R. *Identity Theft*. Upper Saddle River, NJ: Prentice Hall, 2003.

Weisbaum, Herb. "Why ID Theft Insurance Might Not Be Worth It." MSNBC.com. May 8, 2006. www.msnbc.msn.com/id/12692565/ns/business-consumernews.

Weisman, Steve. *50 Ways to Protect Your Identity and Your Credit*. Upper Saddle River, NJ: Prentice Hall, 2005.

"What Are Identity Theft and Identity Fraud?" United States Department of Justice, February 7, 2017. https://www.justice.gov/criminal-fraud/identity-theft/identity-theft-and-identity-fraud.

"What We Investigate: Identity Theft." FBI. Accessed March 7, 2018. https://www.fbi.gov/investigate/white-collar-crime/identity-theft.

White, Jamie. "Yahoo Says Breach Compromised Another 1 Billion User Accounts." LifeLock, December 15, 2016. https://www.lifelock.com/education/yahoo-says-breach-compromised-another-1-billion-user-accounts.

Wilson, Michael R. *Frequently Asked Questions about Identity Theft*. New York: Rosen Publishing Group, 2007.

Wolff, Josephine. "The Real Reasons Why Cybercrimes May Be Vastly Undercounted." *Slate*, February 12, 2018. https://slate.com/technology/2018/02/the-real-reasons-why-cybercrimes-are-vastly-underreported.html.

——. "Why Is the U.S. Determined to Have the Least-Secure Credit Cards in the World?" *Atlantic*, March 10, 2016. https://www.theatlantic.com/business/archive/2016/03/us-determined-to-have-the-least-secure-credit-cards-in-the-world/473199.

Wong, Samantha. "Identity Theft Affects Many in HK, Data Show." *Standard* (Hong Kong), June 23, 2017. http://www.thestandard.com.hk/section-news.php?id=184309.

Worthen, Ben. "New Data Privacy Laws Set for Firms." *Wall Street Journal*. October 16, 2008. https://www.wsj.com/articles/SB122411532152538495.

Zhang, Sarah. "The Loopholes in the Law Prohibiting Genetic Discrimination." *Atlantic*, March 13, 2017. https://www.theatlantic.com/health/archive/2017/03/genetic-discrimination-law-gina/519216.

Zhiliang, Cheng and Li Baojie. "Police Officer's Daughter Enters University in Name of Classmate, Evoking Nationwide Outcry." *China View*, October 5, 2009. http://bbs.chinadaily.com.cn/viewthread.php?tid=637561.

Index

About the Authors

Rachael Hanel has written more than twenty nonfiction books and teaches journalism, English, and history at the college level. She is the author of We'll Be the Last Ones to Let You Down: Memoir of a Gravedigger's Daughter, a finalist for the 2014 Minnesota Book Awards.

Erin L. McCoy is a literature, language, and cultural studies educator and an award-winning photojournalist and poet. She holds a master of arts degree in Hispanic studies and a master of fine arts degree in poetry from the University of Washington. She has edited nearly twenty nonfiction books for young adults, including The Mexican-American War and The Israel-Palestine Border Conflict from the Redrawing the Map series with Cavendish Square Publishing. She is from Louisville, Kentucky.